Vincent

Ingo F. Walther

VINCENT VAN GOGH

1853–1890

Vision und Wirklichkeit

TASCHEN

ABBILDUNG SEITE 2:
Selbstbildnis mit Strohhut
Paris, Sommer 1887
Öl auf Pappe, 41 x 33 cm
Amsterdam, Rijksmuseum Vincent
van Gogh

ABBILDUNG UMSCHLAGRÜCKSEITE:
Selbstbildnis vor der Staffelei
Paris, Januar 1888
Öl auf Leinwand, 65 x 50,5 cm
Amsterdam, Rijksmuseum Vincent
van Gogh

»Ich lebe, um zu malen.«

© Benedikt Taschen Verlag GmbH & Co. KG, Köln 1986
Produktion: Ingo F. Walther, Alling
Mitarbeit und Redaktion: Rainer Metzger, Charly Prestele
Typographie und Herstellung: Ingo F. Walther
    und Hubert K. Hepfinger, Freising
Satz: Wolfgang Hellmich, Moosburg
Farbreproduktionen: Repro Ludwig, Zell am See
Schwarzweißreproduktionen: W. Klüg, Grafing
Korrekturen: Uwe Steffen, München
Herstellung: Kölnische Verlagsdruckerei GmbH, Köln
ISBN 3-8228-0036-8
Best.-Nr. 18/31

Inhalt

Halb Mönch, halb Künstler
Die Anfänge in Holland 1881-1885

Sein Leben war ein einziger Mißerfolg. In allem, was seiner Welt, seiner Zeit belangvoll schien, war er ein Versager: Er war unfähig, eine Familie zu gründen, unfähig, seinen Lebensunterhalt zu bestreiten, ja sogar unfähig, mit Menschen Kontakt zu halten. Doch als Maler fand er ein Mittel, dem Chaos der Wirklichkeit eine — seine — Ordnung entgegenzusetzen. Seine Kunst war das Regelwerk in einer Welt, gegen eine Welt, mit der er augenscheinlich nicht zurechtkam. Ihrer Undurchschaubarkeit hielt er eine gnadenlose, auch theoretisch fundierte Stringenz des Künstlers entgegen, ihrer Anonymität antwortete er mit fein abgewogenem Pathos, ihrem steten Fluß begegnete er mit der Vitalität des einzelnen. Nicht verdrängen wollte er die Wirklichkeit, auch nicht entsagend an ihr leiden, sondern sie verständlich, greifbar werden lassen. Durch die Kunst sollte die ihm so feindliche Welt zu seiner werden.

Erst nach seinem Tod zollte man ihm Anerkennung. Im Geniebegriff fand das bürgerliche Publikum, dessen Wertvorstellungen ihn zeitlebens abstießen, einen Zugang zu ihm und seinem Werk. Vincent, der Ungeliebte, wurde zum Heros, je mehr sich die Kunst als Welt des schönen Scheins etablierte. In den Randzonen der Gesellschaft, in die sich die Kunst seit hundert Jahren eingenistet hat, wird auch der Außenseiter van Gogh zu einer Persönlichkeit: abgehoben zwar, aber exemplarisch das Unbehagen an der Realität verkörpernd, das jeden ab und zu überkommt. Die Moderne kokettiert gern mit dem Bild des vereinsamten, unverstandenen Künstlers. Auch darin war van Gogh beispielhaft. Er ist einer der ersten Märtyrer der Avantgarde.

Der erste Sohn des protestantischen Pfarrers Theodorus van Gogh war eine Totgeburt. Als auf den Tag genau ein Jahr später, am 30. März 1853, seine Frau Anna Cornelia van Gogh erneut ein Kind zur Welt brachte, voller Zweifel und Angst um die Lebensfähigkeit dieses Knaben, erhielt es denselben Namen wie das erste: Vincent Willem van Gogh. Schon seine Geburt also war von dem Dilemma seines zukünftigen Lebens überschattet. Vincents grundlegende Erfahrung war und blieb die des Scheiterns. Die vielversprechende Karriere als Kunsthändler, in den Niederlanden wie auch speziell in seiner Familie von einer langen Tradition begleitet, endete mit seiner Entlassung. Das darauf begonnene Studium der Theologie überforderte ihn, und er brach es nach einem Jahr wieder ab. Darauf versuchte er sich als Hilfslehrer und Laienprediger, verdingte sich im belgischen Kohlerevier der Borinage

Der Sämann
Den Haag, Dezember 1882
Feder und Pinsel, 61 x 40 cm
Amsterdam, Stiftung de Boer

Brustbild einer Bäuerin mit weißer Haube
Nuenen, März 1885
Öl auf Leinwand auf Holz, 41 x 31,5 cm
Zürich, Sammlung E.G. Bührle

unter den Ärmsten der Armen, doch mehr als die tiefgreifende Erfahrung äußersten sozialen Elends blieb ihm dabei nicht; sein spärlicher Lohn wurde ihm bald gestrichen. Seit dieser Zeit war er gänzlich von der finanziellen Unterstützung seines vier Jahre jüngeren Bruders Theo abhängig. Mit der ständigen Angst, die brüderlichen Zuwendungen würden ihm verweigert, lebte er bis zu seinem Tod. Privates Glück blieb ihm ebenso versagt; seine Welt war nicht die der Frauen, um die er sich vergeblich bemühte.

So wurde die Kunst zu Vincents einzigem Ventil. Sie entwickelte er zu dem Medium, in dem er seine Erfahrungen verarbeitete, seine Kommentare abgab, sein Scheitern und seine Hoffnungen artikulierte. Begleitet wurde sie von einem umfangreichen Briefwechsel, vor allem mit Bruder Theo. Gerade Vincents Briefe bezeugen, wie die künstlerische Betätigung immer mehr seine Vorstellung von der Wirklichkeit bestimmte. Und sie dokumentieren auch das hohe theoretische Niveau, mit dem er zu Werke ging. Briefe und Bilder stellen eine paradoxe Einheit in seinem Œuvre her, in dem ein naiv anmutender Mangel an Weltverständnis von großem Reflexionsvermögen begleitet und ergänzt wird.

Van Goghs Entschluß, Künstler zu werden, ist um 1880 endgültig. Durch seine Tätigkeit in den verschiedenen Filialen der Pariser Kunsthandlung Goupil & Cie. mit dem historischen und zeitgenössischen Schaffen von Grund auf vertraut, artikuliert er schon während seines Studiums, vor allem aber in der bestürzenden Zeit als Laienprediger in der Borinage seine Probleme zeichnerisch. Nach dem Scheitern in bürgerlichen Berufen, nach der Zurückweisung auch seiner theologischen und sozialen Ambitionen ergreift er das Naheliegende, ihm theoretisch und praktisch Vertraute. Zusätzliche Bestätigung erfährt er durch seinen Bruder Theo, bei Goupil beschäftigt, und durch seinen Vetter Anton Mauve, Maler in Den Haag. Im Oktober 1880 zieht van Gogh nach Brüssel, schließt dort Freundschaft mit dem Maler Anton van Rappard. Zunächst entstehen ausschließlich Zeichnungen, Detailskizzen und viele Studien nach Bildern von Jean-François Millet. Dessen etwas süßlicher Realismus liefert ihm Themen, die ihm nahestehen: Darstellungen arbeitender Bauern vor allem, Genrebilder in einem dunklen, Melancholie verbreitenden Ton.

Diese Stimmung, die seiner eigenen Gefühlslage zu entsprechen schien, versucht er in die Zeichnung zu übertragen. Er verwendet zunehmend ungebleichtes Ingrespapier als Unterlage und erhält so die Möglichkeit, malerische Werte, verwischte Konturen und fließende Übergänge der Dominanz der Linie, wie sie in der Zeichnung angelegt ist, entgegenzusetzen. Von da an ist der Schritt zur Malerei nicht mehr weit.

Am Neujahrstag 1882 geht van Gogh nach Den Haag und bezieht hier ein von Theo finanziertes Atelier. Unter Mauves Anleitung entstehen die ersten Ölbilder. Stark von der Haager Schule beeinflußt, der Mauve angehört, ist denn auch das frühe Bild »Am Strand von Scheveningen« (Abb. rechts) vom August 1882. Sehr der Tradition verhaftet, versuchte die Haager Schule vor allem in der Landschaftsmalerei das »Goldene Zeitalter« der holländischen Barockmalerei neu zu beleben. Adriaen van de Velde war der barocke Spezialist für Seestücke, und seine Kombination von Landschaftsbild und der Darstellung sich geschäftig am

Alter Fischer
Feder und Bleistift, 43 x 25 cm
Den Haag, Januar 1883
Otterlo, Rijksmuseum Kröller-Müller

Ufer tummelnder Menschen war auch für van Gogh noch verbindlich. »Wenn ich Landschaften machen werde, wird immer etwas Figürliches drin sein«, schrieb er programmatisch; die künstlerische Tradition trifft sich hier also mit seinem eigenen malerischen Konzept. Dennoch enthält das Bild Anlagen zur Autonomisierung von Form und Farbe: In dem pastosen Farbauftrag etwa, in der Betonung der bildparallelen Schichten und in der Variierung der bräunlichen Farbtöne macht sich eine grundlegende Tendenz zur Abstraktion bereits bemerkbar.

Nur durch ein fundiertes Training in der Kunstbetrachtung und einen geradezu manischen Malfleiß erklärbar, steht van Goghs Farbbehandlung, nach nur knapp einem Jahr eigener Malpraxis, schon auf der Höhe der Zeit: Das Problem der Tonmalerei ist ganz aktuell. Auf Beobachtungen von Eugène Delacroix fußend, stellte man sich die Frage, wie die Abänderung der Farbe, die bei einem Gegenstand dann bemerkbar ist, wenn man ihn aus größerer Distanz oder bei anderer Lichteinwirkung betrachtet, malerisch zu bewältigen sei. Die Lösung, die man sich abrang, bestand nun darin, die konkrete Farbe des Gegenstandes, seine Lokalfarbe, zugunsten einer das ganze Bild beherrschenden einheitlichen Färbung, die zu Tönen variiert wird, zu unterdrücken. Nicht mehr die Eigenartigkeit des Gegenstandes wird also betont, sondern seine Erscheinung in dem Zusammenhang, dem man das Bild widmet.

Am Strand von Scheveningen
Scheveningen, August 1882
Öl auf Papier auf Pappe, 34,5 x 51 cm
Amsterdam, Stedelijk Museum

»Wir haben hier in der ganzen Woche viel Wind, Sturm und Regen gehabt, und ich bin oft in Scheveningen gewesen, um es mir anzusehen. Ich habe zwei kleine Seestücke davon mit nach Hause gebracht. Schon in dem einen steckt viel Sand — aber das zweite, als es richtig stürmte und das Meer bis dicht an die Dünen kam, habe ich zweimal vollständig abkratzen müssen, weil es ganz mit einer dicken Sandschicht bedeckt war. Der Sturm war so arg, daß ich mich kaum auf den Füßen halten und wegen des stiebenden Sandes fast nichts sehen konnte.«
VINCENT VAN GOGH

9

Diese hier angelegte Ablösung der Farbe im Bild von der des konkreten Dinges in der Wirklichkeit war der wichtigste Schritt hin zu ihrer gänzlichen Autonomie. Farbe kann nun auch als Phänomen, als reine Erscheinung, als Spiel von untereinander abgestimmten Flecken wahrgenommen werden. Begünstigt auch durch die eigene Tradition, die fortschrittliche Behandlung der Farbe bei einem Rembrandt oder Frans Hals, wird van Gogh in seinem Werk dieser Autonomie neue Dimensionen verleihen. Noch allerdings bewegt er sich im Rahmen des Konventionellen. Noch macht der Ton van Goghs malerische Musik.

Im September 1883 endet der Aufenthalt in Den Haag. Van Gogh zieht — allein — in die Provinz Drente im Nordosten der Niederlande. Vorausgegangen war der Bruch mit seinem künstlerischen Mentor Mauve. Weniger Mauves laute Kritik an Vincents Zusammmenleben mit der Prostituierten Clasina Maria Hoornik, von ihm Sien genannt — sie war ihm Modell und Geliebte in einem —, als grundlegende Differenzen über das Malen mögen dazu geführt haben. In Vincents Augen war Mauve eben Exponent einer akademischen Kunstauffassung, die, von Normen, Regeln und einem strengen Schönheitskanon gegängelt, den individuellen Ausdruck und die aktuellen sozialen Probleme in unzulässiger Weise vernachlässigte. Autoritäten waren ihm von jeher ein Dorn im Auge, und Mauves strikte Ansichten über Kunst mögen ihn aufs fatalste an den bigotten Calvinismus seines Elternhauses erinnert haben. Die alte Haßliebe zu seiner Herkunft brach durch, van Gogh suchte sich ihr durch

Die Staatslotterie
Den Haag, September 1882
Aquarell, 38 x 57 cm
Amsterdam, Rijksmuseum Vincent
van Gogh

Flucht in die Einsamkeit zu entziehen; in eine Einsamkeit freilich, die er nicht ertragen konnte. Nach einem Vierteljahr kehrte er als verlorener Sohn nach Nuenen zu seinen Eltern zurück. Die haben sich mittlerweile mit dem Künstlerdasein ihres ältesten Sohnes abgefunden und stellen ihm in einem Nebengebäude des Pfarrhauses sogar ein Atelier zur Verfügung.

Hier entstand im Mai 1884 der »Weber am Webstuhl« (Abb. S. 13). Vollkommen in seine Arbeit vertieft, sitzt der Weber an seinem Gerät. Monumental baut sich der Webstuhl, fast das ganze Bildformat ausfüllend, im Vordergrund auf. Er wirkt wie ein überdimensionierter Rahmen, der den schmächtigen Körper des Webers mit seinem Gitterwerk aus Horizontalen und Vertikalen, die Gestalt teilweise überschneidend, zum Bestandteil seiner eigenen Mechanik zu machen scheint. Gemeinsam heben sich auch ihre dunklen Silhouetten vor dem hellen Hintergrund ab, den das spärliche Lämpchen nie beleuchten kann. In dieser vereinheitlichenden Darstellung von Arbeiter und Arbeitsgerät ist jedes pittoreske Element, ist jede Anekdote verbannt. Die Härte und

Bäuerin und Bauer beim Kartoffellegen
Nuenen, April 1885
Öl auf Leinwand, 33 x 41 cm
Zürich, Kunsthaus

11

Mühe, aber auch die Würde des Arbeitslebens kommen unverstellt zum Ausdruck.

Das Bild dokumentiert eindringlich van Goghs Solidarität, ja seine Identifikation mit dem Dargestellten. Er war überzeugter Sozialist. Aus eigener Erfahrung kannte er das Elend der Arbeiter, und auch seine eigene Kunstproduktion war ihm Handarbeit. Bauern, Weber und Bergleute waren denn auch bevorzugte Gestalten seines frühen Œuvres: Vertreter des Landproletariats, keine Stadtbewohner, obwohl van Gogh auch deren Leben aus eigener Anschauung, aus London und Paris, kannte. Dies verweist auf seine tiefgreifende Abneigung gegen die Industrialisierung, gegen eine Maschinenwelt, die den Menschen zum Rädchen degradiert. Van Gogh vertrat einen eigenartig pessimistischen Fortschrittsglauben, wie er auch bei den englischen Sozialutopisten William Morris und John Ruskin zum Ausdruck kommt. Das Ideal einer herrschaftsfreien Gesellschaft verband sich hier mit dem Lobgesang auf das Handwerk. Der selbstproduzierende freie Arbeiter, als den sich van Gogh selbst sah, war Brennpunkt seiner sozialistischen Projektionen. Darin unterschied er sich auch von dem in der Zeit so modischen Naturalismus, dessen Exponenten, allen voran der Schriftsteller Emile Zola, mehr die neutrale Schilderung des Arbeiterelends als eine eigene, tätige Anteilnahme betrieben. Die Nobilitierung des Arbeiters, der im Naturalismus Thema der Kunst wurde, ging van Gogh dementsprechend zuwenig weit: Der Arbeiter sollte auch sein Publikum sein. Kunst aus dem Volk für das Volk – dies war der soziale Impetus seines Schaffens. Bilder wie »Die Staatslotterie« (Abb. S. 10) oder »Bäuerin und Bauer beim Kartoffellegen« (Abb. S. 11) sind dafür beispielhaft. Zentrale Figuren dieser Arbeiten sind anonyme Menschen aus dem Volk, Bauern oder Arbeiter, so bildwürdig wie ehedem der strahlende Held aus Geschichte und Mythologie.

Einmal, ein einziges Mal, waren van Goghs Bauern Thema und Publikum zugleich. Mit Unterstützung seines Bruders konnte er von seinen »Kartoffelessern« zwanzig Lithographien drucken lassen, günstig zu erwerben von den Menschen aus der Umgebung. In vielfacher Hinsicht ist dieses Bild (Abb. S. 14) vom Mai 1885 eine Zusammenfassung seines frühen Schaffens überhaupt. Zusammengehörigkeit und Armut drücken sich aus in dem kargen Mahl, das die fünf ausgemergelten, abgearbeiteten Gestalten hier teilen. Kartoffeln und Malzkaffee werden ganz selbstverständlich über den Tisch gereicht, und die neidlose Gemeinsamkeit erreicht ein fast schon religiös wirkendes stilles Pathos.

»Ich habe mich nämlich sehr bemüht«, schreibt Vincent an seinen Bruder Theo, »den Betrachter auf den Gedanken zu bringen, daß diese Leute, die hier bei ihrer Lampe Kartoffeln essen, mit denselben Händen, die in die Schüssel langen, auch selber die Erde umgegraben haben; das Bild spricht also von ihrer Hände Arbeit und davon, daß sie ihr Essen ehrlich verdient haben ... Aber wer die Bauern lieber süßlich sieht, der mag bei seiner Ansicht bleiben.« Aus eigener Kraft scheinen die Gesichter zu leuchten, ihre Würde noch steigernd. Über einem dunklen, in bräunlichen Tönen gehaltenen Hintergrund ergibt sich der Lichteffekt rein aus der Kontrastwirkung durch das spärlich aufgesetzte Gelb. Das Bild entstand nach sorgfältiger Planung und vielen vorbereitenden

Weber am Webstuhl
Nuenen, Februar-März 1884
Feder, 26 x 21 cm
Amsterdam, Rijksmuseum Vincent
van Gogh

Studien, zu denen auch das »Brustbild einer Bäuerin mit weißer Haube« (Abb. S. 6) vom Dezember 1884 gehört. Aus der noch etwas additiven Zusammensetzung vieler Studien zu einem Bildganzen erklärt sich vielleicht auch die unterdrückte Kommunikation der fünf Figuren, ihre verstohlen wirkenden Blicke, die sich kaum zu treffen scheinen. Doch der vermeintliche Mangel in der Komposition verleiht dem Bild auch seine Stille, seine leise Melancholie.

»Du wirst mir recht geben, daß eine solche Arbeit nicht ernst zu nehmen ist. Zum Glück kannst du mehr als das.« Mit diesen Worten kommentierte und kritisierte Rappard das Bild seines Freundes, besiegelte damit auch das Ende seiner Freundschaft zu dem empfindlich verletzten van Gogh. Rappard spielte auf die »Fehler« an, die er, an akademischen Sehweisen geschult, bei den »Kartoffelessern« entdeckte, zu kurz geratene Arme, aufgedunsene Gesichter, schlechte Proportionen. Dabei hatte van Gogh gerade so etwas wie einen eigenen Schönheitskanon entwickelt, orientiert an den Menschen seiner Umgebung, die nicht schön waren, aber seinen Begriff von Wahrhaftigkeit verkörperten.

Weber am Webstuhl
Nuenen, Mai 1884
Öl auf Leinwand, 70 × 85 cm
Otterlo, Rijksmuseum Kröller-Müller

»Was die Arbeit betrifft, so habe ich ein ziemlich großes Bild von einem Weber unter den Händen — der Webstuhl direkt von vorn, die Figur eine dunkle Silhouette gegen die weiße Wand ... Mit diesen Webstühlen werde ich noch viel Not haben, aber sie sind so wunderbar schöne Vorwürfe, all das alte Eichenholz gegen eine gräuliche Wand, und ich glaube bestimmt, es ist gut, daß sie einmal gemalt werden.«
VINCENT VAN GOGH

Die Kartoffelesser
Nuenen, April 1885
Öl auf Leinwand, 82 x 114 cm
Amsterdam, Rijksmuseum Vincent
van Gogh

»Mich bestürzte in diesem Durcheinander
eine Mahlzeit armer Leute in einer unheim-
lichen Hütte unter trüber Lampe. Er nannte
es ›Die Kartoffelesser‹; es war auf grandiose
Weise häßlich und voll beunruhigenden
Lebens.« EMILE BERNARD

Abneigung gegen ein traditionelles Normengefüge, die Solidarität mit
den Armen und vielleicht auch ein tatsächlich vorhandener Mangel an
bildnerischen Ausdrucksmitteln hatten diese Ästhetik kreiert. Van Gogh
hatte sich nach vielen Rückschlägen aufgerafft, hatte sich mit seinem
Künstlertum identifiziert, seine fehlende Begabung durch zähen Fleiß
und Übung ausgeglichen. Kunst war nun individuelles Ausdrucksmittel;
Schönheit und Häßlichkeit waren Kriterien des einzelnen und nicht
Kategorien allgemeiner Übereinkunft. Van Goghs Ästhetik des Häßli-
chen, bereits im 18. Jahrhundert von Edmund Burke und Denis Diderot
theoretisch vorbereitet, ist Charakteristikum seines Schaffens, Deforma-
tionen und grelle Farben bürgen für seine spezielle Qualität. Seine Bildsprache bleibt immer orientiert an der konkreten Wirklichkeit, ist Reaktion
auf sie und persönlicher Kommentar — so persönlich allerdings, daß
anerkannte Regeln sie nur zerstören würden.

Am 26. März 1885 stirbt der Vater Theodorus van Gogh. Von da an
wird Vincents Leben in dem Dorf Nuenen immer schwieriger, die Leute
fürchten sich vor seinem ebenso verschlossenen wie plötzlich aufbrau-
senden Gebaren. Er hatte sie immer gern gehabt, diese Menschen, fühlte
sich als Teil von ihnen, doch verständlich machen konnte er sich nicht.
Der Aufbruch nach Antwerpen wird auch eine Veränderung seiner

Themenwelt mit sich bringen. Das soziale Engagement, das so unverhüllt in den Bildern zum Ausdruck kommt, wird abgelöst werden durch eine zunehmend rein künstlerische Auseinandersetzung: Van Goghs Gegenüber wird sich ändern. Treu allerdings wird er seinem Kampf um Selbstbehauptung bleiben, seinem Aufstand der Gefühle gegen die Kalküle.

Das »Stilleben mit Bibel« (Abb. S. 15), im Oktober 1885 entstanden, kurz vor der Abreise, rechnet mit dem Vergangenen kurzerhand ab. Die Bibel, Symbol für Elternhaus und religiöse Erziehung, hat im Bild einen Konkurrenten, Zolas »La Joie de vivre«, Kultbuch des Naturalismus und für den alten Theodorus eines der schlimmsten Machwerke. Die Kerze, Instrument der Sakralisierung, hebt beide Bücher auf dasselbe Niveau, gibt ihnen die gleiche Bedeutung. Doch ist sie ausgeblasen. In der Großstadt, in Paris, wird van Gogh sich von beiden Büchern distanzieren. Christentum und Sozialismus werden in eine neue Religion einfließen, doch nicht mehr sein Leben bestimmen. Die neue, ausschließliche Religion heißt Kunst.

Stilleben mit Bibel
Nuenen, Oktober 1885
Öl auf Leinwand, 65 x 78 cm
Amsterdam, Rijksmuseum Vincent van Gogh

»Aber den Weg, den ich gehe, muß ich einhalten; wenn ich nichts tue, wenn ich nicht studiere, wenn ich nicht suche, dann bin ich verloren. Dann wehe mir!«
VINCENT VAN GOGH

Lehrjahre in Paris
Antwerpen und Paris 1885-1888

Mit den »Kartoffelessern« in seinem kargen Gepäck kommt van Gogh Ende November 1885 in Antwerpen an. Der belgische Welthafen wird nur Kulisse für ein kurzes Intermezzo sein auf Vincents Weg nach Paris, der Hauptstadt des 19. Jahrhunderts. Dennoch ist der Aufenthalt hier entscheidend für sein späteres Schaffen. Die Zeit des Experimentierens beginnt erst in Antwerpen, der Aufbruch aus der calvinistischen Strenge seiner Heimat, die Loslösung von den bei allem Widerstreben doch prägenden Bindungen an eine vertraute Umwelt setzt erst hier van Goghs kreativen Elan ganz frei. War die Frühzeit seines Schaffens doch von der düster-schwermütigen Welt der Bauern bestimmt, so wird Vincent in den kommenden zwei Jahren alles an künstlerischen Ausdrucksformen durchspielen, was sich zu seiner Zeit ungewöhnlich, fortschrittlich und avantgardistisch gab.

So gut es eben geht, richtet sich van Gogh in der armseligen Kammer ein, die er mit Theos Unterstützung beziehen kann. Bei den Bouquinisten und Antiquaren der Hafengegend erwirbt er für einen Spottpreis japanische Holzschnitte, tapeziert mit ihnen die kahlen Wände seines Zimmers und gewinnt so einen ersten Zugang zu ihrer dekorativen Farbigkeit, die ihn später so nachhaltig faszinieren wird. An der Königlichen Akademie wird er sich im Kopieren von Gipsmodellen antiker Skulpturen üben, doch wie schon in Den Haag fühlt er sich auch hier von dem Dogma antiker Schönheit, von der Reduktion einer persönlichen Handschrift auf mechanische Nachahmung abgestoßen. Wichtiger wird ihm die Bekanntschaft mit Bildern von Peter Paul Rubens, dem Altmeister des Barock, der sein Atelier hier in Antwerpen hatte. Dessen fröhliche Farbigkeit, dralle Formen und üppige Volumen, Kennzeichen der barocken Malerei katholischer Provenienz, erschließen sich ihm als notwendige Alternative zu der zurückhaltenden, kontrollierten Strenge der holländischen Kunst.

Eines Morgens, Anfang März 1886, erreicht Theo die lapidare Mitteilung: »Ich bin ab Mittag im Louvre, oder auch früher, wenn Du willst.« Was Vincent in seinen Briefen aus Antwerpen immer wieder anklingen ließ, damit überrumpelte er seinen Bruder nun. Vincent war in Paris gelandet und gedachte jetzt, mit Theo in eine gemeinsame Wohnung zu ziehen. Theo gab sich widerwillig geschlagen. Viele Reibereien, Eskapaden Vincents und Entschuldigungen Theos werden die folgenden knapp zwei Jahre begleiten.

»Ich habe lieber hundert Francs im Monat und die Freiheit, damit zu machen, was ich will, als zweihundert Francs ohne diese Freiheit.«　VINCENT VAN GOGH

Montmartre nahe der oberen Mühle
Paris, Oktober-Dezember 1886
Öl auf Leinwand auf Masonitplatte,
44 x 33,5 cm
Chicago, Art Institute of Chicago

Eines der frühen Pariser Bilder ist das »Stilleben mit Makrelen, Zitronen und Tomaten« (Abb. unten), entstanden im Sommer 1886. Die Antwerpener Neuerungen finden hier deutlichen Niederschlag: Das knallige Rot der Tomaten in seinem wirksamen Kontrast zu dem Grün des Kruges, überhaupt die Verwendung reiner Farben, die nicht als Grundton das ganze Bild überziehen, weist geradewegs auf Rubens zurück. Und die Verunklärung des Raumzusammenhangs, die verwischte Grenze zwischen Tisch und Hintergrund, die Widersprüche im räumlichen Hintereinander von Tisch, Tomaten und Krug deuten auf die Kenntnis der japanischen Drucke, bei denen das dargestellte Raumkontinuum stets zugunsten ornamentaler Flächigkeit in Frage gestellt ist.

Henri de Toulouse-Lautrec und Emile Bernard waren die vielleicht begabtesten, sicher aber die bekanntesten Absolventen von Cormons Atelier, der Mal- und Zeichenschule des als Künstler unbedeutenden, als Lehrer aber recht erfolgreichen Malers Fernand Cormon. Für drei Monate wird auch van Gogh sie besuchen, dort seine Vorliebe für das Genre, Bauern- und Arbeiterbilder, verlieren und vor allem Kontakte knüpfen eben zu Toulouse-Lautrec und Bernard. Über Theo, der im Zwischengeschoß der kleinen Filiale von Goupil, die er leitete, eine zwanglose Auswahl von impressionistischen Bildern ausstellte, lernt Vincent denn

Stilleben mit Makrelen, Zitronen und Tomaten
Paris, Sommer 1886
Öl auf Leinwand, 39 x 56,5 cm
Winterthur, Sammlung Oskar Reinhart

auch Paul Gauguin, damals genauso unbekannt wie er selbst, und
Camille Pissarro kennen, den schon sechzigjährigen großen alten Mann
des Impressionismus. Sie wird er dann als seine Freunde betrachten,
gemeinsam machen sie die kleinen Cafés und billigen Restaurants in der
Gegend um den Boulevard de Clichy am Montmartre unsicher, wo sie
alle Nachbarn sind. Mit ihnen träumt Vincent den Traum von einer
großen Künstlerkommune, vom freien Arbeiten mit- und füreinander,
gerade mit ihnen auch wird sein Vorhaben scheitern.

    In ein winterliches Grau, in die verschleierte Stimmung aufziehen-
den Nebels taucht van Gogh seine Ansicht des »Montmartre nahe der
oberen Mühle« (Abb. S. 16), die zwischen Oktober und Dezember 1886
entstand. Die kühle Atmosphäre des nahenden Winters hat er ganz im
Sinne des impressionistischen Stimmungsbildes eingefangen, auch die
Neutralität des ganzen Geschehens, die scheinbar teilnahmslos vorüber-
eilenden Passanten, die fragmenthafte Optik des Bildes mit dem über-
schnittenen Aussichtsplateau stehen in der Tradition eines Claude Monet
oder Auguste Renoir.

    Schon im Oktober 1886 malte van Gogh »Das Gartenlokal ›La
Guinguette‹ auf dem Montmartre« (Abb. oben). Auch hier baut er auf

**Gartenlokal »La Guinguette« auf dem
Montmartre**
Paris, Oktober 1886
Öl auf Leinwand, 49 x 64 cm
Paris, Musée du Jeu de Paume

19

einer typisch impressionistischen Sehweise auf. Das zarte Rot des sich herbstlich färbenden Laubes, die spärlich besetzten Bänke im Vordergrund, der Blick in die mit wenigen Pinselstrichen skizzierten Lauben kristallieren einen Augenblick stiller Alltäglichkeit heraus, eine Momentaufnahme ohne tiefere Bedeutung. Daran ändert auch der an einigen Stellen recht pastose Farbauftrag nichts, auch nicht die verstohlenen Stellen von Lokalfarbigkeit, die aus dem herbstlichen Ocker herausfallen. In diesen Bildern experimentiert van Gogh mit dem Impressionismus.

1886, als Vincent in Paris ankam, hatte sich der Impressionismus eigentlich schon überlebt. Edouard Manet, der Stammvater, war tot, und auf ihrem achten Salon, der eben in diesem Jahre stattfand, tauchten schon die Neoimpressionisten auf – Georges Seurat zeigte sein berühmtes »Ein Sonntagnachmittag auf der Ile Grande Jatte« (Chicago, Art Institute). Die scheinbare Teilnahmslosigkeit der impressionistischen Manier, der Verzicht auf einen Ausdruck persönlichen Engagements, die fast mechanische Umsetzung des Seheindrucks in ein spontanes, ad hoc entstandenes Gemälde, all dies wurde nun nicht mehr nur von den Sachwaltern des Ewig-Gestrigen kritisiert, sondern auch von einer selbstbewußten, sich recht genial findenden jungen Generation. Licht war das Zauberwort der Impressionisten, Licht als Träger aller Erscheinungen, Licht als verbindendes, alle Dinge zusammenfassendes Urelement, Licht auch als lebenspendende Kraft. Doch den durchaus gegebenen philosophischen Hintergrund erachtete man für gering. Kein Maler der damaligen Zeit allerdings kam am Impressionismus vorbei. Was letztendlich blieb für van Gogh, für die anderen rebellischen jungen Maler, war die Freude an der Helligkeit, war die Verwendung eines reinen Weiß, waren auch die Ausschnitthaftigkeit, das scheinbar unzusammenhängende räumliche Gefüge.

»Ich male viel lieber die Augen der Leute als Kathedralen.« Mit diesen Worten kommentierte van Gogh die Beliebigkeit des Themas bei den Impressionisten, ein Satz, der auf Monets Kathedralen von Rouen, die Bilderserie von Ansichten dieses Domes zu verschiedenen Tageszeiten, vorauszuweisen scheint. Van Gogh also malte lieber Porträts. Die »Sitzende Frau im ›Café du Tambourin‹« vom Februar 1887 (Abb. rechts) ist denn auch keine Aufnahme einer anonymen verwahrlosten Trinkerin in irgendeiner Kneipe, sondern ein konkretes Bildnis. Dargestellt ist die Italienerin Agostina Segatori, früher Modell unter anderem von Camille Corot und Edgar Degas und nun Besitzerin des Cafés, in dem sie hier am Tisch sitzend porträtiert wird. Vincent war kurze Zeit mit ihr liiert und hat sie häufiger dargestellt, auch als Aktmodell. »Café du Tambourin« heißt ihr Betrieb, entsprechend haben Tisch- und Stuhlplatten die Form des Schelleninstruments. Überhaupt ist der exotische Reiz der Darstellung, die eigenartige Frisur der Frau und ihr Folklorekleid, dazu der Fächer auf dem Stuhl und die japanischen Holzschnitte im Hintergrund, viel zentraler für die Bildaussage als das verräucherte Milieu irgendeiner Spelunke, das Degas bei seiner »Absinthtrinkerin« (Paris, Musée du Jeu de Paume), augenscheinlich Vorbild für van Gogh, so faszinierte. Die großen melancholischen Augen der Frau in einem fremdartigen Ambiente verleihen dem Bild eine spezielle, genau bedachte Stimmung, die das Gegenteil der anonymen Atmosphäre darstellt, wie sie die Impressionisten lieben.

Sitzende Frau im »Café du Tambourin«
Paris, Februar 1887
Öl auf Leinwand, 55,5 x 46,5 cm
Amsterdam, Rijksmuseum Vincent van Gogh

»Peintres du Petit Boulevard« nannte van Gogh ironisch die Maler-
clique, die mit ihm am Montmartre wohnte, arbeitete und auch ausstellte.
Alle lebten sie recht einfach, richteten sich in der Abgeschiedenheit von
den großen Prachtstraßen ein, glichen mangelnde Bekanntheit mit
Experimentierlust aus. In einem Restaurant am Boulevard de Clichy,
dem »Du Chalet«, hatten sie 1887 ihre erste Ausstellung: van Gogh,
Toulouse-Lautrec, Bernard und Louis Anquetin. Verkauft wurde nichts,
aber die Präsentation begleiteten lange Diskussionen, und zu guter Letzt
tauschten sie ihre Werke einfach untereinander aus. Ihre ärmliche Kunst-
idylle hatte genau den bohemehaften Schick, der die Künstler aller
Länder in Paris vereinigte. Sie lebten, ihres Genius bewußt, in dem
unbedingten Vertrauen, bald die Kunstwelt zu revolutionieren.
　　Ausflüge konnten sie sich nur in die nächste Umgebung leisten.
Gemeinsam mit Gauguin und Bernard verbrachte van Gogh viele Tage
in Asnières, einem beliebten Badeörtchen an der Seine. Hier malt er auch
im Sommer 1887 »Die Seine mit der Brücke ›Grande Jatte‹« (Abb. oben).
Die sich diagonal durch das Bild schiebende Brücke war ein häufig
wiederkehrendes Motiv der Impressionisten, oftmals einfach vom
Rahmen überschnitten und so auch das Momenthafte der Aufnahme

Die Seine mit der Brücke »Grande Jatte«
Paris, Sommer 1887
Öl auf Leinwand, 32 x 40,5 cm
Amsterdam, Rijksmuseum Vincent
van Gogh

**Stilleben mit Flasche und Zitronen
auf einem Teller**
Paris, Frühjahr 1887
Öl auf Leinwand, 46 x 38 cm
Amsterdam, Rijksmuseum Vincent
van Gogh

Vier Sonnenblumen
Paris, Sommer 1887
Öl auf Leinwand, 60 x 100 cm
Otterlo, Rijksmuseum Kröller-Müller

zum Ausdruck bringend. Van Gogh nimmt hier darauf Bezug. Doch der auf den ersten Blick wirr erscheinende Farbauftrag in horizontalen, vertikalen und diagonalen Strichen, der völlige Verzicht auf Farbflächen bei gleichzeitiger Betonung der Farbintensität suchen auf die gleiche Art und Weise das Strahlend-Atmosphärische zugunsten zeitloser Beherrschtheit zu überwinden wie die gleichzeitigen Werke des Pointillismus.

Die Inkunabel dieses Malstils ist Seurats »Ein Sonntagnachmittag auf der Ile Grande Jatte«, das van Gogh schon im Thema des Bildes zitiert. Seurat und seine Freunde, allen voran Paul Signac, wollten den Impressionismus auf eine sozusagen wissenschaftliche Ebene stellen. Bis zum Rand angefüllt mit Theorien über Farbschwankungen, Volumenwirkungen und Wahrnehmungspsychologie suchten sie aus der Manier des Impressionismus objektive Gesetze zu destillieren, vor allem auch ihre Bilder danach auszurichten, für ihre Kunst die gleiche Objektivität der Darstellung zu fordern wie für ihr theoretisches Programm. Van Gogh, mit Signac gut bekannt, ging bei aller Neigung zur Kunsttheorie dieser naturwissenschaftliche Zugang doch zu weit. Aber die Methode, Farben in Tupfen zu zerlegen, die erst bei distanzierterer Betrachtung eine ständig in Bewegung scheinende Fläche ausbilden, lag gerade im Rahmen seiner Experimentierlust. Noch in den schwermütigen Gemälden seines Spätwerks wird diese Farbzerlegung Gültigkeit haben. Die »Vase mit Margeriten und Anemonen« (Abb. S. 26) vom Sommer 1887 jedenfalls zeigt, vor allem in der Gestaltung des Hintergrundes, die Faszination jener Striche und Tupfer auf van Gogh: eine flirrende Folie, vor der selbst die überquellende Buntheit der Blumen recht seriös wirkt.

24

Daß ihm auch andere malerische Ausdrucksformen zur Verfügung stehen, beweisen die zur gleichen Zeit entstandenen »Vier Sonnenblumen« (Abb. links). Die vier ausgedörrten Blüten, monumental nah gesehen, stecken an längst abgeschnittenen dürren Stengeln. Als wollten sie sich gegen die drohende Verrottung aufbäumen, spreizen sie ihre kurzen Blütenblätter von sich, wie Flammen züngelnd, schon das ekstatische Emporlodern von van Goghs späten Zypressen vorwegnehmend. Dem banalen Allerweltsmotiv gewinnt Vincent hier fast existenzielle Aussagekraft ab, die Gegenstände werden zu Symbolen, Chiffren irgendeines Leidens, das man am ehesten beim Maler selbst zu suchen hat. Zunächst ist diese vitalisierende Sicht der Dinge auch Reaktion auf die Fotografie: »Man erstrebt eine tiefere Ähnlichkeit als die des Fotografen«, schreibt der Maler an seine Schwester. Doch wichtiger ist der dekorative, symbolisierende, unmittelbar ansprechende Effekt, den die Erscheinung des Bildes, losgelöst von allen Motivvorlagen aus der Wirklichkeit, hervorruft. Ein Effekt, der nichts hat von dem kultivierten Raffinement des Impressionismus, sondern der spontane Anteilnahme, ja Betroffenheit fordert und dies alles hervorrufen will durch die kraftvolle Inszenierung einer simplen Sonnenblume.

Garant dafür ist in erster Linie der Komplementärkontrast zwischen dem schmutzigen Gelb und dem schillernden Blau des diffusen Hintergrunds. Lange schon hatte sich van Gogh mit den Farbtheorien von Delacroix beschäftigt. Wichtigste Erkenntnis daraus war für ihn — neben dem Gedanken der Farbautonomie — der Einsatz des Komplementärkontrastes. Dieser Kontrast ergibt sich, wenn man eine der drei Grund-

LINKS:
Japonaiserie: Blühender Pflaumenbaum
(nach einem Holzschnitt von Hiroshige)
Paris, Sommer 1887
Öl auf Leinwand, 55 x 46 cm
Amsterdam, Rijksmuseum Vincent
van Gogh

RECHTS:
Japonaiserie: Brücke im Regen
(nach einem Holzschnitt von Hiroshige)
Paris, Sommer 1887
Öl auf Leinwand, 73 x 54 cm
Amsterdam, Rijksmuseum Vincent
van Gogh

»Ich beneide die Japaner um die ungemeine, saubere Klarheit, die alle ihre Arbeiten haben. Nie ist das langweilig, und nie scheint es zu sehr in Eile gemacht. Das ist so einfach wie Atmen, und sie machen eine Figur mit ein paar sicheren Strichen mit derartiger Leichtigkeit, als wäre das genauso einfach, wie seine Weste zuzuknöpfen.«
VINCENT VAN GOGH

farben – Gelb, Rot, Blau – der Mischung aus den anderen beiden gegenübergestellt. Die Kombinationen Rot – Grün, Gelb – Violett, und Blau – Orange steigern sich gegenseitig in der Intensität ihrer Farbigkeit oder neutralisieren sich zu einem unscheinbaren Grau, wenn man sie vermischt. Dieser scheinbar so banale Trick konnte doch eine oftmals geradezu ekstatische Farbwirkung hervorrufen.

Alles auf einmal wollte sich Vincent in seiner Pariser Zeit aneignen. Es war, als wollte er die Vielfalt der Ausdrucksformen, die der Schmelztiegel Paris nicht nur in der Kunst in sich vereinte, in seinem einzigen Medium, der Malerei, richtiggehend nachleben. Vielfalt an Ausdrucksmitteln bestimmt auch das »Stilleben mit Flasche und Zitronen auf einem Teller« (Abb. S. 22) vom Frühjahr 1887. Die harten, festen Formen des Obstes sind hier umgeben von einem fein skizzierten Grund, angelegt in radialen Linien, die die Kontur des Tellers aufgreifen. Das rötliche Gelb der Früchte und das grünliche Blau des Untergrunds stehen dabei in Komplementärkontrast. Ganz in impressionistischem Sinn brechen sich daneben Farben und Licht in der transparenten Helligkeit der gerippten Flasche. Hinterlegt ist das Arrangement von dem dekorativen Liniengefüge einer Tapete. Sie nun weist auf ein weiteres wichtiges Feld künstlerischen Ausdrucks hin, das van Gogh in dieser Zeit aufgriff: auf den Japonismus, damals weit über die bildende Kunst hinaus eine verbreitete Modeerscheinung.

Bereits 1867 hatte auf der Pariser Weltausstellung der Pavillon Japans großes Aufsehen erregt. In neuer Weltoffenheit bewunderte man die exotische Fremdheit, den dabei dennoch augenscheinlich hohen Grad an Zivilisiertheit der fernöstlichen Kultur. Plötzlich tragen die Damen der besseren Gesellschaft Fächer, behängen sich mit Kimonos, holen sich Porzellangeschirr und Wandschirme in ihre feudalen Wohnungen. Die Warenhäuser legen sich eine Japan-Abteilung zu. Eine veritable Mode war geboren. Die Reaktion der bildenden Kunst ließ nicht lange auf sich warten. Holzschnitte aus Japan, billig nachgedruckt oder sorgfältig importiert, galten plötzlich als stilbildend. In ihren festen Konturen fand man eine passende Antwort auf die Auflösung der Formen im Impressionismus, in ihrer dekorativen Farbigkeit eine Reaktion auf die triste Inszenierung des Elends durch den Naturalismus.

Japonaiserien nennt man Kopien nach japanischen Holzschnitten. Von van Gogh sind drei solcher Imitationen bekannt. Sein »Blühender Pflaumenbaum« folgt ebenso wie die »Brücke im Regen« (Abb. S. 25) Vorlagen von Hiroshige, der als einer der letzten berühmten Meister fast ein Zeitgenosse war. Japanische Holzschnitte des 19. Jahrhunderts zeigen bereits Berührungspunkte mit westlicher Kunst, gerade sie also waren für eine Übernahme besonders geeignet. Bei aller versuchten Nachahmung sind van Goghs Versionen dennoch weit von ihren Vorbildern entfernt. Der Farbauftrag erreicht nie die flächenbezogene Glätte Hiroshiges, im Gegenteil, die pastose Farbigkeit van Goghs betont eine persönliche Handschrift, statt sie zu nivellieren. Auch das Bildformat hat er verändert, den schmalen Bildstreifen durch Bahnen mit japanischen Schriftzeichen, deren Bedeutung er sicher nicht kannte, verbreitert. Kurz, van Gogh hat die Vorlagen europäisiert, sie seiner eigenen Bildsprache so angepaßt, daß sie dem aktuellen Trend entsprachen.

»Maler ist er, Maler bleibt er; ob er, noch jung, Holland ins Dunkle übersetzt, ob er, etwas älter, als Divisionist Montmartre und seine Gärten malt oder schließlich durch wütenden, pastosen Farbauftrag den Süden oder Auvers-sur-Oise wiedergibt. Ob er zeichnet oder nicht zeichnet, ob er sich in Farbflecken oder in Entstellung verliert, Maler bleibt er immerdar.«
EMILE BERNARD, in: ›Mercure de France‹, 1893

Vase mit Margeriten und Anemonen
Paris, Sommer 1887
Öl auf Leinwand, 61 x 38 cm
Otterlo, Rijksmuseum Kröller-Müller

Der Farbenhändler »Père« Tanguy
Paris, Winter 1887/88
Bleistift, 21,5 x 13,5 cm
Amsterdam, Rijksmuseum Vincent
van Gogh

Gegen Ende seiner Pariser Zeit malte Vincent drei Porträts seines Farbenhändlers, des alten Julien Tanguy, von allen nur »Père« Tanguy genannt. Er hatte noch die große Zeit der Verwirklichung sozialistischer Ideale miterlebt, die Tage der Pariser Kommune, mußte deswegen ins Exil gehen, galt aber den Künstlern als Grandseigneur ihrer eigenen Utopien. Sehr billig und oft auf Kredit erhielten sie bei ihm ihr Malmaterial, und in einem Nebenraum hatte Tanguy eine kleine Galerie eingerichtet, von der das große Publikum keine Notiz nahm. Père Tanguy ist fast eine Schlüsselfigur der Moderne, waren doch in seinem Hinterzimmer van Gogh, Seurat, Gauguin und Paul Cézanne mit Bildern vertreten, jene vier Maler also, die man später als Wegbereiter des 20. Jahrhunderts apostrophieren wird. Nirgendwo anders als bei Tanguy lernten sie gegenseitig ihre Arbeiten kennen. Von Cézanne ist auch eine Bemerkung über die Bilder van Goghs überliefert. Er nannte sie kurzerhand »Werke eines Verrückten«.

Das Porträt von Père Tanguy (Abb. rechts) nun faßt van Goghs Pariser Schaffen ähnlich souverän zusammen wie die »Kartoffelesser« das niederländische. Streng frontal, fast symmetrisch ist der alte Herr wiedergegeben, monumental sitzt er im Vordergrund des Bildes. Diese vereinfachende Darstellung steht im Kontrast zu dem komplizierten Gefüge des Hintergrundes, der tapeziert ist mit japanischen Holzschnitten. Extrem flach wirkt das Ganze, die japanischen Tänzer scheinen geradewegs an die Figur vorne zu stoßen. Genau die Nivellierung des räumlichen Zusammenhangs ist hier bemerkbar, die auf eine Illusion der konkreten Wirklichkeit verzichtet.

Van Gogh wird dieses Prinzip weiter ausbauen, der Weg wird für ihn so frei sein zur Wiedergabe anderer Realitäten, seiner eigenen Innenwelt, die sich so oft schon vehement geltend gemacht hatte. Farbe und Pinselführung werden seine entscheidenden Ausdrucksmittel sein. Die Helligkeit des Impressionismus, die Auflösung von Flächen zu grafischen Strukturen durch den Pointillismus, die dekorative Flächigkeit des Japonismus, eben diese Prinzipien hat sich van Gogh in den beiden Jahren in Paris angeeignet, in ständiger Auseinandersetzung mit seinen Künstlerkollegen. Mit ihnen hat er die Farbtheorien von Delacroix diskutiert und den Gebrauch des Komplementärkontrastes, die rigide Verwendung der Farbe Schwarz und auch den zunehmenden Verzicht auf Lokalfarben vervollkommnet. Die Theorien gingen ihm in Fleisch und Blut über, Komposition und Farbgebung waren bald kein Akt mehr überlegter Setzung, sondern spontaner Geste vor der Leinwand. Die Pariser Zeit war van Goghs lernfähigste, er lehnte Akademien ab, aber je mehr ihm die Kunst zum Lebensinhalt wurde, um so mehr Kenntnisse erwarb er sich im Kontakt mit seiner kunstbeflissenen Umgebung.

So fühlte er sich bereit, jenen Weg zu gehen, den vor ihm vor allem schon Cézanne beschritten hatte. Er wollte in den Süden, wo die Natur, die er für seine Studien so benötigte, freundlicher, das Licht heller, die Farben intensiver waren. Auch schien eine Trennung von seinem Bruder geraten, der durch Vincents Eskapaden bereits Schwierigkeiten mit seinem Arbeitgeber bekommen hatte. So hoffnungsvoll, wie sein Naturell es zuließ, bestieg Vincent van Gogh am 20. Februar 1888 den Zug nach Arles.

Bildnis des Farbenhändlers »Père« Tanguy
Paris, Winter 1887/88
Öl auf Leinwand, 65 x 51 cm
Athen, Sammlung Stavros S. Niarchos

Die Explosion der Farbe
Arles 1888-1889

Der Sog des Südens: Spätestens seit Albrecht Dürers Italienreise zog es die Maler des Nordens ans Mittelmeer. Es waren nicht allein die Architektur und Malerei des Quattrocento, die es zu entdecken galt, das erhebende Gefühl, geschichtsträchtigen Boden zu betreten, es war auch die Faszination der mediterranen Landschaft mit ihrem milden Klima, von der warmen Sonne in ein strahlendes Licht getaucht, die die Künstler in Scharen lockte. Die Auswirkungen dieses »Künstlertourismus« ließen die Bilder spüren: Die Paletten werden bunter, die Farben heller, die Themen antikischer. Paul Klee hat das Erlebnis des Südens mit seinem emphatischen Bekenntnis geschildert, mit dem er das Ergebnis seiner Tunisreise zusammenfaßte: »Ich habe die Farbe entdeckt.«

Doch warum gerade Arles? Degas verbrachte einmal einen Sommer hier. Adolphe Monticelli, Maler pastoser, farbenfroher Blumenstilleben und für van Gogh bei den langen Auseinandersetzungen mit seinen Pariser Kollegen eine Art grauer Eminenz, lebte ganz in der Nähe, in Marseille. Zola wurde in der Gegend geboren, in Aix-en-Provence, dem Ort, wo Cézanne seit langem lebte. Außerdem hieß es, die Frauen von Arles seien die schönsten der Welt. Van Gogh selbst erwähnt keinen konkreten Grund für seine Wahl. Die Abreise im Februar jedenfalls war auch eine Flucht vor der tristen Melancholie des Pariser Winters.

»Ich habe hier japanische Kunst nicht nötig, denn ich rede mir vor, daß ich in Japan bin und nur meine Augen zu öffnen und zu nehmen brauche, was ich vor mir habe«, schrieb van Gogh kurz nach seiner Ankunft an die Schwester. Wie um sich selbst in der Richtigkeit dieses Satzes zu bestätigen, wählte er für die ersten in Arles entstandenen Bilder die japanischsten Motive überhaupt. Der »Blühende Pfirsichbaum« (Abb. S. 35), gemalt im März 1888, stand ihm als Objekt konkret vor Augen. Mehr noch aber als die Freude auf den nahenden Frühling, den das Bäumchen so unmißverständlich ankündigt, drückt van Gogh die Befriedigung aus, daß ihn seine Hoffnung auf ein Fernost vor der Haustür nicht trog. Statt vor einem Holzschnitt Hiroshiges, wie in Paris, kann er nun seine Japanvisionen vor der Wirklichkeit selbst ausleben. Der blühende Baum, durch Zäune vor dem Mistral des Mittelmeers geschützt, steht stellvertretend für van Goghs eigenen Optimismus, wird zum Symbol seiner eigenen Wünsche und Projektionen.

Für fünf Francs am Tag, damit eigentlich über seine Verhältnisse lebend, hat sich van Gogh in einem Restaurant eingemietet. Das kleine

»Jetzt, da ich das Meer hier gesehen habe, fühle ich ganz, wie wichtig es ist, im Süden zu bleiben und zu spüren, daß man die Farbe bis zum Alleräußersten treiben muß — es ist nicht mehr weit bis Afrika.«
VINCENT VAN GOGH

Zwölf Sonnenblumen in einer Vase
Arles, August 1888
Öl auf Leinwand, 91 x 72 cm
München, Neue Pinakothek

Mansardenzimmer, das er bewohnt, ist als Atelier ungeeignet. Er kennt niemanden, der ihm Modell stünde, und so wird die Gegend um Arles, Bäume, Hügel, Brücken, Fischerhütten, zum einzigen Bildmotiv. Die Camargue, das sumpfige, im 19. Jahrhundert noch weitgehend unkultivierte Delta der Rhone, die Ebene der Crau mit ihren Weizenfeldern und Weinbergen und der Strand um den Wallfahrtsort Saintes-Maries-de-la-Mer gleichen den Nachholbedarf an Natur aus, der sich in den zwei Jahren der Großstadt angesammelt hat. Bei den weiten Spaziergängen will Vincent auch seine angegriffene Gesundheit wieder in Ordnung bringen, hat er doch durch Alkoholismus, übermäßigen Tabakkonsum und mangelhafte Ernährung permanent Raubbau an seinem Körper getrieben.

Vielleicht fühlte er sich an die holländische Heimat erinnert: Jedenfalls zog es ihn immer wieder an den Kanal südlich von Arles, um die Brücke und ihre Umgebung zu studieren. Die beiden gemalten Fassungen der »Brücke von Langlois« (Abb. unten und rechts) entstan-

Die Brücke von Langlois bei Arles mit Wäscherinnen
Arles, März 1888
Öl auf Leinwand, 54 x 65 cm
Otterlo, Rijksmuseum Kröller-Müller

of the opposite-facing bridge in contre-jour light, of persons on the bridge recognizable only as shadows, in addition the light, white-toned application of colour, are all reminiscent of the Impressionists' techniques which most obviously influenced van Gogh here. The early version is completely different. The artist is standing directly on the banks of the canal. Objects now stand out sharply against the lofty horizon and have the appearance of radiating colour from themselves, mainly due to the use of red tonality combined with all the colours. Here the directed, participating, binding view geared towards the concrete object makes itself felt; a technique which Vincent was to cultivate gradually during his Arles period.

In so doing van Gogh developed a new form of tone painting, which excels that of his master Delacroix. Autonomy of colour and tone painting are one here. Just as before, the colouring of the picture arises out of the play on varieties of one specific colour and tones – the only difference now being that this basic colour no longer corresponds to reality. A rich yellow, a gaudy red now rise above the mere task of portraying an appearance. Colour alone is the means of expressing

Drawbridge with Lady with Parasol
Arles, May 1888
Oil on canvas, 49,5 × 64 cm
Wallraf-Richartz-Museum, Cologne

Drawbridge with Lady with Parasol
Arles, May 1888
Pen, 23,5 × 31 cm
County Museum, Los Angeles

oneself individually, as well as portraying the idea of reality present in the artist's psyche. Light and shadow, reflections and refractions of colour are deliberately subdued, but these qualities of the painting still have their pictorial origin in actual perception and not in mere imagination. A certain colour is no longer chosen because it corresponds to the actual, but because it is able to strengthen the vehement nature of expression. This colour is no longer objectively verifiable, but only subjectively understandable.

Still there is little reason for such vehemence of expression. On the contrary, paintings such as "Harvest Landscape" (p. 36) of June 1888 take complete pleasure in what is seen. Here van Gogh painted a typically traditional landscape scene, indeed he used a richer intensity of colour, but it is clearly close to reality in the toned-down colour of the delicate blue in the background.

After just having moved, Vincent looked for another cheaper room in a café and at the same time he rented a house, his famous "yellow house", which he gradually furnished. At least from May onwards he had studios at his disposal and a place to store his numerous new paintings. He was still completely optimistic at this time.

Once a year the small fishing village Saintes-Marie-de-la-Mer becomes the centre of gypsies in Europe. On the 24th May they meet here to honour their patron saint, St. Sarah, and take part in the pilgrimage. The whole region is in complete turmoil, thronging full of half-fearful, half-curious people. Naturally van Gogh's interest was stirred. His excursions to the area around Arles came to an end with his journey to the Mediterranean coast. "Fishing Boats on the Beach" (p. 37), painted at the beginning of June 1888, takes up and reworks a theme from the earlier period: the beach scene. Now the sea is literally pushed to the edge of the painting and its atmospheric blue is barely marked off by the line of the horizon from the similar composition of the sky, and thus is a mere piece of scenery for the graphic exactness of the thing itself. With an almost dissecting accuracy of observation, van Gogh is fully engrossed in the material nature of the banal motif, in the surging movement of the hull and the tilted intricacy of the mast. Van Gogh presents things almost lovingly – boats, vases, chairs, shoes, creating a visible panorama.

The autonomy of colour does not go hand-in-hand with the autonomy of form. The form of an object, its contours and surface composition remain in his work true to reality all of the time: "It's true I turn my back completely on nature, when I transform a sketch into a painting, decide upon the colours, enlarge or simplify, but in relation to the actual form I am afraid of moving too far away from reality and thus of not being exact enough." This he admitted in a letter to the artist Bernard. He continues: "I don't in fact invent the whole painting, on the contrary, I discover the thing, but it must come out of nature." Van Gogh approaches things which he will later use in his pictures not by making quick sketches but by drawing in more exact detail. The concrete motif remains his constant foundation and corrective of his representations,

Peach Tree in Bloom
(Im memory of Mauve)
Arles, March 1888
Oil on canvas, 73 × 59,5 cm
Rijksmuseum Kröller-Müller, Otterlo

Harvest Landscape
Arles, June 1888
Oil on canvas, 72,5 × 92 cm
Rijksmuseum Vincent van Gogh,
Amsterdam

"An endlessly flat landscape – seen from a bird's eye view from the top of the hill – vineyards, harvested corn fields. All this is multiplied to infinity and spreads like the surface of the sea to the horizon, which is bordered by the hills of Crau."

VINCENT VAN GOGH

over which colour is then placed like a second skin, which van Gogh chose solely according to its effect in the painting. In this way the dignity of the object therefore remains intact.

Thus the red-haired eccentric lived amongst the people of Arles: taciturn, introverted, added to the fact that as an artist he was considered as having no respectable profession, constantly in need of money, and saddled with an unpronounceable name, a fact which van Gogh had taken into account early on by signing his works with his Christian name only. So it was almost half a year before he was able to make close friends with the people he admired and whose portraits he could paint. Portrait painting was van Gogh's way of examining in an artistic light the people, friendship and affection which were so often denied him in life. He himself said that the art of portrait painting "lets me develop that which is the best and deepest within me". The colours thus become increasingly the means by which characters are depicted, as well as becoming more and more independent of the concrete externalities of the object portrayed. In a certain sense, the people he painted were all,

like himself, outsiders. Strangely enough, he never painted a portrait of his brother Theo, not even during his time in Paris.

"Zouave Milliet Seated" (p. 39), portraying an infantry soldier from Algeria and painted at the end of June 1888, is van Gogh's first portrait since that of "Père" Tanguy. "I've finally found a model," rejoiced van Gogh about the African who was on holiday in Arles. Milliet, the name of the soldier, later characterized van Gogh accurately in his remark: "This young man who shows both talent and good taste in his drawings becomes abnormal as soon as he touches a brush." As always this portrait was not commissioned. His main reason for painting this portrait was the exotic appearance of the man in his unusual traditional costume, which reminded him of Delacroix' models, whom the latter came across in Morocco. A strange contradiction between spatiality and flatness is typical of this depiction. The perfectly-captured natural facial expressions stand all the more to the fore due to the decorative patterning of the clothing, contrasting with the pastose colouring behind. The tiled floor appears to slip away towards the forefront of the picture, leading to

Fishing Boats on the Beach
Arles, June 1888
Oil on canvas, 64,5 × 81 cm
Rijksmuseum Vincent van Gogh,
Amsterdam

"Spent a week in Saintes-Maries . . . on the really flat sandy beach with small green, red and blue boats, which in their form and colour are as pretty as flowers. One man alone uses them. These skiffs rarely ever go on the high seas. They set off when there is no wind blowing and return to land as soon as the wind becomes too strong." VINCENT VAN GOGH

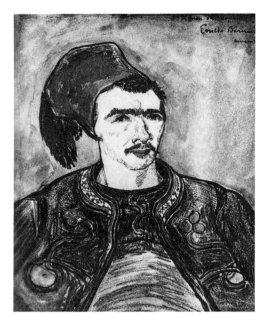

Zouave Milliet (Half-Figure)
Arles, June 1888
Black chalk, pen, watercolour, 30 × 23 cm
Metropolitan Museum of Art, New York

"I've finally found a model – a Zouave – a small chap with a bull's neck and tiger's eyes; I began a portrait and then began a second one . . . the uniform is of the same blue as the enamel pans, with faded orange-red braid and two stars on his chest; a common blue, which was very difficult to get exactly right."

VINCENT VAN GOGH

Zouave Milliet Seated (Whole Figure)
Arles, June 1888
Oil on canvas, 81 × 65 cm
Lasker collection, New York

the model's rather precarious posture.

The few people who van Gogh portrayed during this time appear to have been pushed into a framework in order to maintain an unbroken artistic style. This fact alone points to the impossibility of these portraits having been commissioned. The originality of those portrayed is stressed in their faces, which are all the artist tries to capture exactly; the posture, clothing, application of colour, and composition are in contrast more the result of wanting to create a decorative effect, which is not dependent upon contradictions but which only becomes apparent when colour is applied. Van Gogh was proud of the fact that he deliberately painted his portraits in a hurry: "One must strike while the iron is hot," he wrote and thus adapted his style to the quick gestures of the caricaturist, above all Honoré Daumier. Out of this wish to work quickly one can explain the by-and-large expansive backgrounds and the ornamental play of the colours of the clothing, which appear to be totally apart from the bodies of the persons portrayed.

"La Mousmé" (p. 40) and "The Postman Joseph Roulin" (p. 43) were painted shortly after each other in the summer of 1888. La Mousmé, whom van Gogh described as "a Japanese girl, in this case one from the provinces, 12 or 14 years of age" and Joseph Roulin as "having a head like Socrates" are both sitting in the same easy chair which was in van Gogh's "yellow house". The chair appears too large for the girl, whose slight frame is swamped by the wickerwork of the chair. The country postman, in contrast, sits erect, but appears ill-at-ease in his attempt to accommodate himself comfortably amongst the confinement of the furniture. The girl's skirt and the man's uniform are not so much mere articles of clothing, but rather great ornamentally-worked areas of colour. The faces, in contrast, are finely painted. The shy, nervous glance of the child and the choleric, bloated face of the adult make the concrete appearance of the ordinary people from the neighbourhood comprehensible. These portraits are dedicated to portraying the theme which had so fascinated him in his early works: simple people from the area, captured by the intense observation of the artist who feels at one with them.

Throughout the whole of the summer, van Gogh was occupied with a problem which had troubled his fellow artists for centuries, of how one should portray darkness using colour when painting night scenes. How could one make colour, which only comes alive when in contrast with light, flexible so that the opposite, darkness, is portrayed? Van Gogh appears to have found the key to this problem on a walk at night along the seashore. "It wasn't cheerful, it wasn't sad, it was just – beautiful," he wrote, deeply moved, to Theo afterwards. This atmosphere, gained by sparse light in front of a dark horizon, he wanted to portray in his paintings.

Mainly in order to get used to working by artificial light, he painted "The All-Night Café" (p. 44/45) in September 1888. For four days or so he slept only during the day, returning at night to the depressive milieu of the dive which he wanted to paint: lonely drunks cowering behind their

tables, a billiard player, a couple cuddling in the corner, and a waiter – a cast of characters enacting despair. "I have tried," Vincent commented on his painting, "to portray with red and green this terrible human suffering. The room is blood red and dull yellow, a green billiard table in the middle, and four lemon-coloured lamps radiating an orange and green aureola light. Struggle and antitheses are present everywhere: in the completely opposite colours (the greens and reds), in the crouching sleeping figures of the night, in the empty, depressing room, in the violet and blue." And elsewhere Vincent remarked: "I attempted to convey the idea that the café is a place where one can ruin oneself, become crazy or criminal." This painting is one of the few which solely portrays the motif of a pessimistic feeling of life. The café, a place where "one can ruin oneself", get drunk and spend one's last penny, is to follow van Gogh through the last few years of his life up until his own collapse.

The night atmosphere in this painting comes out more through its association with loneliness, suffering and desperation than through the portrayal itself. Only the yellowish aureoles around the lamps point to the fact that the picture was painted at night. Yet "The All-Night Café" is still only a stepping stone, an étude of night painting.

A short time afterwards, with his painting entitled "Café Terrace at Night" (p. 47), van Gogh dared to take the final step into the open. Beneath the starry sky the terrace appears brightly lit up, its reddish yellow is a complementary contrast to the dark blue of the twilight. A strong pull into the black centre of the painting, recognizable by the virtually parallel receding lines above the lintel in the front, pergola and house gables, set off the inviting light of the café in addition to its dark ambience. The light spots of stars in the sky, added to the complementary contrast which is difficult to achieve by sparse light, makes the representation of a night scene quite matter-of-fact.

To paint outdoors was a 19th century achievement. To paint by artificial light was already in the Baroque period a favoured artistic way of passing the time. But to paint outdoors at night by artificial light was van Gogh's very own invention. In this way he presents a crass contrast to the light painting of the Impressionists, stressing a precision of observation in his portrayal of dimly-lit objects, to which the technique of painting outdoors is perfectly suited. "The night is livelier and richer in colour than the day," van Gogh exclaimed enthusiastically. The vaguely recognizable things spur on the depiction of exactness and fantasy. Van Gogh continues to use the technique of painting at night throughout the remaining few years of his life, his greatest achievement being "Starry Night" (p. 68).

Van Gogh's painting of his "Yellow House" (p. 49) of September 1888, although not a night painting, keeps to the same colours as the above mentioned work. Shortly after he had rented the house in May, van Gogh had it painted yellow, which was an important and symbolic colour for him. Yet for a long time it stood completely without furniture, due to the fact that he had no money to furnish it. Only when Theo sent him 300 francs was he able to afford sparse furnishings. He finally moved

"La Mousmé", Seated in a Cane Chair
Arles, July 1888
Oil on canvas, 74 × 60 cm
National Gallery of Art, Washington

"La Mousmé" (Half Figure)
Arles, June 1888
Pencil and pen, 32,5 × 24,5 cm
Pushkin Museum, Moscow

REPR. P. 42:
Postman Joseph Roulin
Arles, August 1888
Pencil, 31,5 × 24 cm
H. R. Hahnloser collection, Berne

REPR. P. 43:
**Postman Joseph Roulin,
Seated in a Cane Chair**
Arles, July 1888
Oil on canvas, 81 × 65 cm
Museum of Fine Arts, Boston

"In my painting of the 'All-Night Café' I've tried to express the idea that the café is a place where one can ruin oneself, become crazy and criminal. Through the contrast of delicate pink, blood red and dark red, of mild Louis-XV and Veronese green against the yellow-green and stark blue-green tones — all this in an atmosphere like the devil's inferno and pale sulphurous yellow . . . I've tried to convey the sinister power of such a place."

VINCENT VAN GOGH

The All-Night Café
Arles, September 1888
Oil on canvas, 70 × 89 cm
Yale University Art Gallery,
New Haven (Conn.)

Café Terrace at Night
Arles, September 1888
Reed pen, 62 × 47 cm
Emery Reves collection, Roquebrune

"A café in the evening, seen from the outside; on the terrace little figures are seated drinking. A gigantic yellow lamp lights up the terrace, the house fronts and the pavement, and casts out its light onto the street cobbles, which take on a pink-violet colouring. The house façades in the street, under a blue starry sky, are dark blue or violet, in front a green tree. There you have it – a night painting without having used the colour black, only beautiful blue, violet and green, and in this setting the lit-up café takes on a pale sulphurous yellow and lemon colouring."
VINCENT VAN GOGH

Café Terrace at Night
Arles, September 1888
Oil on canvas, 81 × 65,5 cm
Rijksmuseum Kröller-Müller, Otterlo

in in the middle of September. Now he felt like his own master – security and freedom appeared guaranteed thanks to his "ownership", added to the possibility of finally founding the long-awaited artist commune. Out of sheer joy he painted all the houses yellow in his painting, as if they were all at his disposal. For a short while the "yellow house" symbolized everything which appeared important to him and which guaranteed him happiness. The "yellow house" was a personal symbol to him.

At the end of the century Symbolism was an attitude of mind which was to confront van Gogh again and again, especially with regard to his artistic and private disagreement with Gauguin. "The aim of painting and literature," Edouard Dujardin wrote in 1886, himself one of the chief theoreticians of Symbolism, "is to reproduce the discovery of things with the common means of painting and literature. What one should express is not the image, but the character." Symbolism spread like a fashion wave through the young generation of Bohemian artists. The aim was "to portray the essence of the chosen object and in so doing avoid mere photographic imitation."

Van Gogh's painting "Twelve Sunflowers in a Vase" (p. 30) of August 1888 attempts to portray this very essence. With extreme precision he has captured the flowers, yet the pastose application of colour, the confused arrangement of outstretched leaves, and the inner luminosity of the light blue background, give the portrayal a significance which goes far beyond that of the mere painting of the flowers. These sunflowers stand for the artist's imagination, for his identification with them, for some form of deeper meaningfulness, and they appear to have influenced him. "A watering can, a harrow left in the fields, a dog in the sun, an ugly churchyard – all these things can become a receptacle of my revelation. Each of these objects and thousands of other similar ones, which one normally merely glances over with indifference, can, for me personally, at any one moment – but in no way controlled by myself – take on an exalted and stirring character." With these words Hugo von Hofmannsthal characterizes the power of imagination in his "Chandos-Letter".

It was exactly this wish to empathize with the most banal of worldly objects which was to repeatedly inspire van Gogh. The ecstatic movement of the plants in his painting "Majolica Jar with Branches of Oleander" (p. 52) points to the same arbitrary search for a world behind the objects. However, artistic Symbolism as represented by a Dujardin or a Hofmannsthal was always the conscious, deliberate demonstration of an artistic genius, the display of an omnipotent fantasy, which set the artist apart from the commonness of the world. Van Gogh's power of imagination, however, came from his innermost self. It was an expression of a vehement will, a flood of emotion, which later was to contribute to his mental derangement. The worlds portrayed in his paintings are much more self-explanatory, more immediate than the often affected exoticism and esoteric meanings of the Symbolist movement. Van Gogh was not an aesthete influenced by the spirit of that time.

The Yellow House
Arles, September 1888
Reed pen, 13 × 20,5 cm
N. Dreher collection, Brienz

"Now we're experiencing a glorious heat wave without any wind – that just suits me. A sun, a light, which for lack of a better word can only be called yellow, pale sulphurous yellow, pale lemon gold. Oh, how lovely this yellow is."

VINCENT VAN GOGH

A major pictorial means of Symbolism was the framing of all the objects by a common contour. Thus one was able to express the uniqueness of the object which had inspired the artist's imagination, or even the final vagueness of the things, which was necessary in order to make symbols out of them and to stylize them so that they go beyond being mere symbols. Dujardin called this method of painting "Cloisonnism", derived, on the one hand, from mediaeval goldsmith's art, on the other hand, as was always the case then, from Japanese woodcuts.

Van Gogh's "L'Arlésienne" (p. 51) of November 1888, a portrait of Madame Grinoux, the owner of the station café in Arles, is a perfect example of this Cloisonnism. The back of the chair, the table top, and the woman's figure are all embraced by a single contour, which emphasized the silhouette. Van Gogh works the contrasting colour effects into the spacious graphic framework. The depiction is completely flat and details come alive entirely from the line of colour. Van Gogh explains his Cloisonnism thus: "The areas which are surrounded by contours, whether present or not – but in any case tangible – are then filled out with simplified tones."

Cloisonnism was the trade mark of the "Pont-Aven School", whose mentor was Gauguin. He almost dogmatically surrounded surface area with framing lines. They were his guarantee against the mere copying of

reality. Van Gogh, in contrast, views the whole less strictly. His contours, mostly varied in colour, came to the surface, or remained below the surface according to need, since the effect of the picture as a whole, and not a theoretical concept, determined their usage. Gauguin's criticism of van Gogh's inexactitude in this area was one of the reasons which led to their later disagreement.

In the painting "The Trinquetaille Bridge" (p. 56) of October 1888, van Gogh almost completely renounces the use of colour. Thus the effect of the painting becomes subordinate to the contrasting play of linear interweavings on the left-hand side and the larger calmer surface on the right. This view of the bridge over the Rhone – the river itself is not shown in the picture – is based in its lack of colour on his earlier Dutch work, but the motif points to the work done in Paris. Yet the extreme distortion of the area and the confused perspective of the picture point to his later years. The steps in the forefront are drawn uncontrollably into the back of the picture, into the hole, which blocks out the underpass thereby serving as a contrast to the precarious equilibrium of the steel

The Yellow House
Arles, September 1888
Oil on canvas, 76 × 94 cm
Rijksmuseum Vincent van Gogh,
Amsterdam

"My house here is painted butter yellow on the outside and has solid green window shutters; it is located directly in a square with a green park full of plane-trees, oleanders and acacias. And inside all the walls are painted white and the floor is tiled in red. Yet the most striking thing is the glaring blue sky. Inside the house I can really live and breathe and think and paint."   VINCENT VAN GOGH

**L'Arlésienne Madame Ginoux
with Books**
Arles, November 1888
Oil on canvas, 90 × 72 cm
Metropolitan Museum of Art, New York

bridge, which threatens at any time to collapse. One can call it expressivity of space: this constant fragile balance, this precarious ease. Was van Gogh therefore the first Expressionist? His handling of space suggests the answer is yes.

Van Gogh's treatment of colour leads to a similar conclusion. It is primarily representative of his means of expression. Pictures such as the two versions of "The Sower" (pp. 54 and 55) of June and November 1888, were in their intensity of colour, in their courageous use of colour and in the vehemence of colour application unparalleled at that date. The enormous pastose disc, representing the sun, immerses the whole background, the sky, in a rich yellow. The front of the picture, the soil, is covered in a hazy blue, shimmering violet: a total reverse of the colours in reality. The real yellow field becomes blue, the real blue sky yellow. The only decisive factor is the contrasting effect of colours.

However, these pictures are in no way abstract. All of them stick to concrete reality as a foundation which is covered by colour as a means of the artist's expression. Here lies van Gogh's actual expressiveness. He presents a detail from everyday life and at the same time an interpretation by means of colour and composition. And this interpretation only when in contrast with the concrete appearance exposes the vehemence of his expressive will and the temperamental artistic gesture. A second reality, artistically pure and subjective, pushes the first aside.

"As long as people work like people with their heart and soul, aiming to do their best, it doesn't matter how bad they are at their job, a certain priceless something attaches itself to manual work," was Ruskin's apologia on craftmanship. Van Gogh too was concerned with manual work on canvas, which only then made sense of the whole. He was the first artist to use an individual expression, favoured by Ruskin, rather than apparently perfect handling, expressive gestures rather than academic beauty in his work, not as a conscious pictorial interpretation of the theoretician, but as a common view acquired in his daily use of colour and brush. The dignity of the individual as a creative being was a moral view. The problem which Ruskin and van Gogh had to cope with – the former theoretically, the latter in practice – was that expression does not also mean the conveyance of a message, but in fact freedom of artistic gesture is the first step in breaking down the public's understanding.

The indifference which confronted van Gogh throughout his life and thus also in Arles meant that positive stimuli became increasingly rare. The fund of stimulating themes, the landscape, some portraits had long been exhausted. The artistic debate with his fellow artists, which had kept up his spirits in Paris, was missing in the enclave of the province. Challenges for his work came less and less from his environment. This environmental reality was such an important stimulus to him. Van Gogh clung more and more to the single utopia, which art left him: the old ideal of a free, self-contained artists' commune. This utopia had been fulfilled for a long time by Gauguin. Founding together with him the "Atelier du Midi", which was supposedly to precede an institute, where

**Majolica Jar with Branches
of Oleander**
Arles, August 1888
Oil on canvas, 60 × 73 cm
Metropolitan Museum of Art, New York

Bernard, Seurat, and Signac would also be involved, became the predominant single theme of his letters written in Arles. All the pictures which van Gogh painted from that summer on indicate this anticipation: they were to decorate the "yellow house", their shared studio, and were to be the starting point and basis for fruitful artistic debates. Gauguin was really going to come. Thus the "Arles tragedy" takes place, mostly understood to be the cause for van Gogh's breakdown. The grotesquerie with Gauguin begins.

The prologue to the whole: Roughly at the same time as van Gogh, Gauguin left Paris. Gauguin did not retreat to the south, instead to the less-expansive, scenically more wild, but according to him unspoilt Brittany. Here he lived in the village of Pont-Aven, continually threatened with debts, occasionally sought out by his friends, more or less taking each day as it came. He felt himself to be an undiscovered genius, but had the same wish as van Gogh – to found an artists' circle. He thought of Bernard, of Anquetin, but never of van Gogh as members

of this artists' circle. As a far-off goal he dreamed of France's colony Martinique, in the far-away tropics where he would find his real fortune. But the shortage of money was his only handicap.

Theo van Gogh exhibited Gauguin's works at his gallery. With his increasing debts Gauguin became more and more dependent on Theo's financial support, just as Vincent was in far-away Arles. Vincent was to use Gauguin's misery to his own purpose and forced his brother to incite Gauguin to come to Arles. In Vincent's mind Gauguin was already with him. Gauguin hesitated to move in with this eccentric whom he did not value highly as an artist. Added to this he mistrusted Theo: "However much Theo likes me, he would definitely not agree to support my living in the Midi only because of my beautiful eyes. He studied the terrain with the cold eyes of a Dutchman and contemplated the view of following the thing as far and as exclusively as possible," Gauguin wrote in October 1888 to Bernard. Gauguin believed Theo's motives were geared towards a business ruse.

Park with a Couple and a Blue Fir Tree
Arles, October 1888
Oil on canvas, 73 × 92 cm
Private collection, USA

53

Sower with Setting Sun (After Millet)
Arles, June 1888
Oil on canvas, 64 × 80,5 cm
Rijksmuseum Kröller-Müller, Otterlo

"However, the painter of the future will be a colourist, such as has never yet existed. Manet was working towards it, but as you know the Impressionists have already got a stronger colour than Manet. This painter of the future – I can't imagine him doing the rounds of the local dives, having false teeth and frequenting the Zouave brothel like me." VINCENT VAN GOGH

Gauguin's feelings of resentment put Vincent even more in a flurry. He thought his humble abode in Arles was not attractive enough for Gauguin. He began to buy furniture, only the best and most comfortable for Gauguin, he himself was content with a modest bed and the smallest room. The whole of van Gogh's paintings bore the mark of Gauguin's expected arrival. He painted a series of sunflower paintings (p. 30), a yellow-in-yellow study, as decoration for the "yellow house". The decorativity of van Gogh's paintings of this period lies in the banal fact that they are no other than mere pieces of decoration rather than works of art. They were intended to document van Gogh's artistic standard, as a starting point for a painting competition with Gauguin, but were to be no more than pieces of furniture. Van Gogh vehemently hurried to paint beautifully.

After all, he attached great importance to Gauguin: "Everything which he does has something soft, calming, amazing about it," van Gogh wrote at the end of May, "people do not understand him yet and he is suffering because he has not sold anything – just like other true poets."

54

In Gauguin's honour he named his depiction of the park in Arles "The Garden of the Poet" (p. 53). It was to hang in a prominent place in Gauguin's room. Yet still there was no trace of Gauguin. Again and again he postponed his departure, which people were constantly forcing him to undertake, finding excuses in letters and financial loop-holes in order to justify his hesitancy. Then finally after Theo had finished paying all his debts, Gauguin arrived in Arles in the early hours of the morning of the 23rd October.

The catastrophe: van Gogh felt on top of the world. He gladly let Gauguin take the lead-role in art, placing himself in the role of the student, who, however, wanted to show what he had learnt. They worked out a lot of motifs together, compared their results and argued over artistic concepts. Van Gogh was much too impulsive, impatient and too tied to the arbitrariness of the fantasy for the considered tactician and rationalist Gauguin, who in December 1888 cried out: "He is a romantic, I myself tend to the primitive. In applying colour he loves the impulsive, whilst I hate disorderly undertakings." For a while van Gogh

Sower with Setting Sun (After Millet)
Arles, November 1888
Burlap on canvas, 73,5 × 93 cm
E. G. Bührle collection, Zurich

"This man will either become mad or else leave us way behind."   CAMILLE PISSARRO

The Trinquetaille Bridge
Arles, October 1888
Oil on canvas, 73,5 × 92,5 cm
Blinkhorts-Kramarsky collection, New York

"The Trinquetaille bridge with all those steps was painted on a grey morning; stone, asphalt, cobbles, everything is grey, the sky is a pale blue, the figures colourful, a sickly small tree with yellow foliage." VINCENT VAN GOGH

appeared to bow to Gauguin's theories; he outlined all areas and did not work any more according to nature, instead the abstraction of "painting from the head" took over. He set himself to using Gauguin's artistic ways, just as he did in Paris, until it reached mere imitation. But now he was too certain of his own talents: "At that time the abstract appeared very inviting to me. But, oh dear, it is a bewitched land! And one is soon confronted by a wall," he tried to explain to Theo. Gauguin's way was simply not his own.

Their collaboration was not to continue for much longer. Gauguin felt himself to be a victim of a game of intrigue between the two brothers; he suspected they wanted to belittle his artistic meaning. Van Gogh himself was disappointed that his honest will to subordination and his willingness to learn found no recognition. Though it was only differences of artistic questions at first, the effect on their pride and understanding of themselves was not long in coming. Gauguin complained to Theo: "The incompatibility of both our characters means that Vincent and I cannot

live together peacefully. It is imperative that I leave."

Vincent saw his entire dream shatter and felt his utopia of an artists' commune, which he had wanted to try out with Gauguin, finally disappear. As symbols of loneliness he painted his and Gauguin's chair in December (above). They both stand vacant, metaphors for the artists who have now departed from where they previously had chatted to one another. Van Gogh's more modest wooden chair with the pipe and tobacco pouch as elemental symbols contrasts with Gauguin's more elaborate arm chair with candle and book, indicative of learning and ambition. Van Gogh painted his chair yellow and violet, which at that time were symbolic of daylight and hope, as seen in the painting the "Yellow House". Against this the red and green colours present a complementary contrast in the painting of Gauguin's chair, just like the red-green of the "All-Night Café" picture which documents darkness and lost hope. Day and night stand opposite one another in the two artists, and also as alternatives of a future life. Gauguin, as the message appears to convey, illuminated the night for van Gogh.

"Ever since I wanted to leave Arles, he has been behaving so strangely that I hardly dare to breathe. 'You want to leave,' he said to me and as soon as I answered in the affirmative he tore a piece, containing the following sentence, from the newspaper: 'The murderer has fled'," Gauguin was later to recall in a letter. Gauguin as a murderer, a murderer of hope and trust. Van Gogh really appeared to be going mad. More than once he got up in the middle of the night and crept to

LEFT:
Vincent's Chair with Pipe
Arles, December 1888
Oil on canvas, 93 × 73,5 cm
Tate Gallery, London

RIGHT:
Gauguin's Chair with Books and Candle
Arles, December 1888
Oil on canvas, 90,5 × 72 cm
Rijksmuseum Vincent van Gogh, Amsterdam

Gauguin's room to see whether he was still there. It was van Gogh's illness that kept Gauguin in Arles: "In spite of a few differences I can't be angry with a good chap who is ill and suffering and calling for me."

But on 23rd December the threatening situation escalated. Gauguin went for a walk in the evening, and van Gogh, suspicious as ever, followed him. Gauguin, who heard the familiar steps approaching nearer and nearer, turned around and looked straight in van Gogh's disturbed face. Van Gogh was supposedly holding a razor blade in his hand. Gauguin spoke softly to Vincent, who then turned around and went back home. Gauguin, disturbed by the whole incident, spent the night at a hotel. When he returned to the "yellow house" the next morning, the whole of Arles was already up on its feet. Van Gogh, plagued by hallucination, had cut off one of his ears with the razor blade which Gauguin claimed to have seen earlier in van Gogh's hand. After van Gogh had temporarily managed to stop the bleeding, he wrapped the lacerated ear in a handkerchief and ran with this to the town brothel in order to give it to a prostitute. As if nothing had happened he returned home and slept. In this state the police, who had by this time been informed, found him. He was then taken to the town hospital.

Meanwhile Gauguin left secretly. In order to quiet his bad conscience he later wrote in his autobiography that van Gogh had threatened him with a knife. In a letter to Bernard, shortly after this 23rd December, he never even mentioned this episode. One can assume that van Gogh did not want to hurt Gauguin that evening; rather, he only wanted to soothe the latter's suspicion. Gauguin used the whole episode as a long-awaited excuse to justify his finally leaving Arles. The way Gauguin got out of the whole affair, without even seeing Vincent one last time, does not put him in a particularly good light.

The epilogue: Vincent stayed in the hospital for fourteen days. Back in his studio he painted the result of the catastrophe: his "Self-Portrait with Bandaged Ear" (right). The whole of the right side of his face is covered by a large, wide bandage which adds a sad seriousness to the artist's almost rigid appearance. Inside a thick coarse cape he appears to be seeking protection from a hostile environment. The gay colour of a Japanese woodcut frames the left side of his face – a stark contrast to the whiteness of the bound wound. Yet the normality of an uncontrolled work, which the woodcuts, reminiscent of the "Père" Tanguy portrait, attest, is lost. The episode with Gauguin was truly an experience which made him realize his own limits.

Van Gogh is no longer his old self. The loneliness which he had to learn to accept in the years previous, as the price for the formation of an artists' commune, was not to leave him in future. "I don't dare to ask other painters to come here after what has happened. They risk losing their mind, just like me," he wrote with resignation in February 1889 to his brother. In his last remaining year he is to experience a loneliness partly chosen, but also one which is forced upon him.

Four weeks after his discharge from the hospital, van Gogh has to

Self-Portrait with Bandaged Ear
Arles, January 1889
Oil on canvas, 60 × 49 cm
Courtauld Institute Galleries, London

**View of Arles. Orchard in Bloom
with Poplars in the Forefront**
Arles, April 1889
Oil on canvas, 72 × 92 cm
New Pinakothek, Munich

"The more ugly, older, more
cantankerous, more ill and poorer I
become, the more I try to make amends
by making my colours more vibrant, more
balanced and beaming." VINCENT VAN GOGH

return again. Signs of persecution mania appear, and he begins to imagine that someone wants to poison him. A petition signed by the inhabitants of Arles seals his final internment. The resentment against van Gogh, which has always been present in spite of his search for recognition, now leads to his complete avoidance of any form of contact with people. This resentment drove him out of Holland and made his stay in Paris difficult. Looked after by a priest and a doctor, he lived until the beginning of May both as patient and prisoner in the Arles hospital. In addition to this he was worried about Theo's marriage in Paris. Vincent now was afraid of losing his one-and-only confidante.

In order to escape the constraints of the asylum he again began painting. Paintings such as "View of Arles. Orchard in Bloom with Poplars in the Foreground" (above) and "The Courtyard of the Hospital in Arles" (right), both of April 1889, may not give a direct hint of the utter desperation felt by him during this time. They document more banal happenings of daily life than his suffering. However, a claustrophobic atmosphere is conjured up in these paintings: the confinement of the

hospital courtyard, which despite the splendid flowers blocks out the view of the distant horizon, and the withered poplars, which thrust themselves like iron bars in front of the town panorama, present an impassable barrier between the artist's position and the object of his dreams – the town and its freedom.

Van Gogh came to terms with his situation very quickly. The world, to which he clung and which piece by piece was taken away from him, did not accept his religious, political and artistic commitments, and he resolved not to bother it any longer. He entered the mental hospital of his own free will, but against the wishes of his brother, whom Vincent tried to prepare for this decision: "I have tried to get used to the idea of starting afresh, but at this present time it is impossible for me. I am afraid of losing my ability to work, which is now coming back to me, if I take on too much and get bogged down with the idea of opening a new studio. And so I wish to stay here for a while, both for my own peace of mind, as well as for that of others."

On 8th May 1889 Vincent moves to Saint-Rémy.

The Courtyard of the Hospital in Arles
Arles, April 1889
Oil on canvas, 73 × 92 cm
Oskar Reinhart collection, Winterthur

"It is enclosed in a courtyard as found in Arabic buildings, bathed in white. In the centre is an old garden with a pond and eight flower beds full of forget-me-nots, Christmas roses, anemones, wall flowers, margueritas etc. And beneath the archways are orange trees and oleander. All in all a picture of flowers and spring green."
VINCENT VAN GOGH

61

Painting as Life
Saint-Rémy and Auvers 1889–1890

"To suffer without complaining is the only lesson one should learn in this life," van Gogh wrote in May 1889 to his brother, Theo, although he had every reason to wrangle with his fate. At the age of 36 Vincent went of his own accord into the Saint-Paul-de Mausole nursing hospital for the mentally ill near Saint-Rémy-de Provence, 17 miles from Arles.

His hopes and plans for the future were completely destroyed. The incurable illness became more and more prominent, and the attempt by the locals of Arles to have him put away lay heavy on his heart. He felt disgarded by society, and Theo's approaching wedding left him fearful of losing the support of his helpful, beloved brother, added to the failure of his most desirous dream, a communal "studio of the south", which was shattered upon Gauguin's departure.

The insight "that I finally feel incapable of taking a new studio and of staying there alone, neither here in Arles, nor anywhere else . . . I would like to stay temporarily in the asylum, because of my own peace of mind as well as that of others", was hard-won, although he had long ago broken with all conventions. There was nothing left for him to do but to accept his situation: "I am ready to play the role of a madman, although I have not at all the strength for such a role." Despairing, he clung to his brother: "If I didn't have your friendship, I would be driven to suicide without giving it a second thought, and cowardly as I am I would do it in the end."

The asylum, where van Gogh spent almost a year, was about two

"I painted a large picture of the village church – the building has a violet appearance against a flat, deep blue sky of pure colour; the stained glass windows are like ultramarine coloured spots; the roof is violet and orange in parts. At the front is something green in bloom and pink coloured sun-burnt sand. It is almost like the studies I made of the old towers and cemetery in Nuenen – the only difference now being that the colour is more expressive and richer."

VINCENT VAN GOGH

The Church in Auvers
Auvers, June 1890
Oil on canvas, 94 × 74 cm
Musée du Jeu de Paume, Paris

Irises
Saint-Rémy, May 1889
Oil on canvas, 71 × 93 cm
Joan Whitney Payson Gallery of Art,
Portland (Maine)

miles from Saint-Rémy in a somewhat lonely district, surrounded by cornfields, vineyards and olive groves – motifs which appear again and again in his paintings. Judging from the dark hallways and barred windows of the cheerless rooms, life in the mens' quarters must have been very depressing for him.

The patients were completely left alone, since the director of the asylum, Dr. Peyron, who ruled it with rigorous thrift, just kept the patients alive and neglected to actually help them; he was not even a specialist in mental illnesses. Van Gogh, apart from twice-weekly baths, also received no medical attention. Yet his life was more bearable in every sense than that of the other unhappy patients. He was allowed to withdraw, to read and work, and to leave the asylum accompanied.

Van Gogh was diagnosed as suffering from epileptic fits. Periodically he suffered from fits of unpredictable length, going through a nebulous stage, followed by a period of blank; in between these periods he was perfectly normal as far as his behaviour was concerned. This normally lasted two to four weeks; the fits came more or less suddenly

Green Wheat Field with Cypress
Saint-Rémy, June 1889
Oil on canvas, 73,5 × 92,5 cm
Národni Gallery, Prague

and with quite a long time span between each new attack. During these attacks he normally became violent and suffered from terrible hallucinations. Every normal activity, such as writing and painting, was impossible during this time. Vincent viewed his own illness quite clearly and from an amazing distance. He accepted the unavoidable: "It consoles me that I can look upon my madness more and more as an illness like any other and thus accept it as such." In his letters to his brother he tried to hide how horribly depressing it was for him to have to live with the mentally ill and paranoid.

However, the ordered and monotonous life in the asylum contributed greatly to his regaining self-respect. He was now also allowed to go into the surrounding area and paint, accompanied by a guard. He set his whole hopes on this; his work alone was capable of dragging him out of his deep depressions. However, his fits did not leave any trace whatsoever in his work, since his periods of illness and those of

"It is only too true that a lot of artists are mentally ill – it's a life which, to put it mildly, makes one an outsider. I'm alright when I completely immerse myself in work, but I'll always remain half crazy."
VINCENT VAN GOGH

Cypresses
Saint-Rémy, June 1889
Pen and reed pen, 62,5 × 47 cm
Brooklyn Museum, New York

"The cypresses constantly occupy my thoughts – I want to paint something similar to my sunflower paintings. It's amazing that nobody has yet painted them as I see them; in their lines and proportions they are as beautiful as Egyptian obelisks. And the green is such a special fine tone. The cypress is a black mark in a sun-filled landscape, but it is one of the most interesting black tones, and I can't think of any other tone that was as difficult to capture. One has to see the cypresses here against the blue, or more correctly *in* the blue."   VINCENT VAN GOGH

Two Cypresses
Saint-Rémy, June 1889
Oil on canvas, 95 × 73 cm
Metropolitan Museum of Art, New York

artistic creativity were strictly kept apart.

Painting became an activity which directly connected him with life. The pictures painted during this period often give the impression of a hyper-intensity which does not stem from illness, that is only in so far as he was possessed with a crazed creativity in the times between his fits. It was as if he wanted to make up for lost time. These pictures also document his attempts not to give up, to avoid renewed attacks by working unendlessly and thus give vent to his intense feelings.

One of his first paintings done in Saint-Rémy is close to his flower paintings of Arles: "Irises" (p. 64). He came across this motif of voluptuous irises on his way to Dr. Paul Gachet's flat. The painting is crammed with the ripe, moist excesses of nature. The deep blue of the finely-drawn iris buds contrasts sharply with the bold green of the leaves with their lancet tongue-like form, which divide the flowers into horizontal rows. The warm red of the soil firmly anchors the plants to the bottom of the picture, while the light green of the flowering meadow takes hold of the flowers from behind. As a stark contrast to all the colourfulness is a large open white iris to the left and at the far right of the picture is a pale blue iris which serves as an echo to the former.

In order for the eye correctly to take in this brilliant display of flowers and arrange them accordingly, the canvas is divided up into different areas of colour, all of which – as in the flow of nature in summer – radiate light from within themselves, thereby creating a balanced, connected harmony. Thus the rich display of colour and variety of forms are not confusing; on the contrary, they support the lively movement of nature. The detail in the painting confirms this view – it is as if the artist had bent down to the flowers. The detail stands for the whole; nature is meant here, the principle of life.

Van Gogh was concerned most of all with getting as close to nature as was possible. Throughout his life this direct, near-erotic relationship to nature had been present: "It is not so much the language of painting as that of nature which one must listen to." To capture this liveliness was his primary aim in painting, which ought to plumb the "roots or the origin of the thing." Van Gogh wanted to penetrate as deeply as possible into life and feel at the same time the very beating of its heart.

As an ideal means of representation he had discovered colour and the actual life present within the colours themselves. He used colours in such a way that they took on a life of their own and thus were ideally suited to show optically the principle of life. His experimentation with colour never arose out of any particular technique of painting, but rather was a wrestling to find an adequate means of portraying a spiritual concern. Everyday objects around him were similes of life, and it was actually this that van Gogh wanted to express in his paintings. Colour had taken on an immediate representational value for existence, for life itself.

Van Gogh was repeatedly concerned with truthfulness in his depiction of human life. He allowed himself only one guideline: reality itself, a contemporary, modern one and not one of a distant past. One

Wheat Field with Cypresses
Saint-Rémy, June 1889
Black chalk, pen, reed pen on paper,
47 × 62 cm
Rijksmuseum Vincent van Gogh,
Amsterdam

could not achieve this by merely copying reality; what counted for van Gogh was what was behind reality. He recognized a "rationale in the mysterious" and so "all reality was at the same time a symbol" – a religious way of viewing things.

One can clearly recognize this religious reality in his paintings, and the complaining, critical, caricature touches are missing in his work. His stance to all things portrayed in his paintings is that of a loving person who accepts reality for what it is. He wanted to reach out to those people who accept the elemental things of life, such as nature, objects, people, pain, joy, duration, transitoriness . . .

A new philosophy of life was born which no longer saw the world through an earthly vale of tears and was not even a simple denial of a higher principle of life this side of the grave. He confronts the primaeval powers of existence, which he found in nature and out of which his natural mysticism arises and makes itself known in his paintings.

His total dedication to nature can be seen in his painting "Green

Wheat Field with Cypress" (p. 65). Here one's gaze is drawn towards the waving greeny-yellow of the ripe wheat field, which flows diagonally across the painting like a great river. The same yellow can be seen in the straw roofs of the houses in the background and also in the cloud formations and the bushes to the top right of the painting. The dark blades of grass in front of the wheat field heighten the movement to the right. Opposite is a massive upright blackish-green cypress pointing upwards – a strong accentuation of colour admidst all the dynamic movement of the painting. Green coloured areas frame the yellow wheat field, against which the light blue of the sky acts as a contrast. This contrast is toned down by the white of the ears of wheat and that of the clouds, so that in spite of the movement one is given the impression of harmony and organized unity.

Colour is still very much a dominant means of expression, yet is no longer the leading force in these paintings, as was the case with the paintings done in Arles; now only a few paintings show large areas of

Wheat Field with Cypresses
Saint-Rémy, June 1889
Oil on canvas, 72,5 × 91,5 cm
National Gallery, London

"There are endless corn fields under dull skies, and I've not shied away from portraying this sadness and utter loneliness . . . I believe these pictures will tell you what I am not able to express in words – namely that which I view as healthy and inspiring in rural life."
VINCENT VAN GOGH

Olive Orchard
Saint-Rémy, June 1889
Oil on canvas, 72 × 92 cm
Rijksmuseum Kröller-Müller, Otterlo

"I can tell you from the beginning that everyone will say that I work too quickly. Don't believe it. It is the excitement, the honesty of a man of nature, led by nature's hand. And sometimes this excitement is so strong that one works without noticing it – the strokes of the brush come in quick succession and lead on from one to the next like words in a conversation or letter. Yet one should not forget that it was not always so and that in the future too many despondent days without any inspiration will follow."

VINCENT VAN GOGH

colour or weighty complementary contrasts. The vividness of colour is now transferred to the forms, or to be more exact, to their movement. This is also seen in the cypress painting.

And yet another new theme is seen here: the cypress, which from now on is to become his central motif. It appears again in the painting "Wheat Field with Cypresses" (above), only here the cypress is pushed to the right-hand side of the painting and appears much darker and longer against the strange colour of the overcast sky – it is the only vertical accent in the picture. The overripe cornfield is wedged between the green areas, surrounded by rising blue cliffs. An ascending diagonal movement leads from the fields over the trees to the hills and from there to the clouds. Their convulsive shapes, only barely indicated here, dominate the whole sky in the later "Starry Night". One could also call this painting "Calm before the Storm". A feeling of calm indeed still pervades the picture, yet a stormy turbulence (of the brushstrokes too) is clearly present.

These evergreen trees become the single theme of the painting "Two Cypresses" (p. 67), which take up almost the whole of the left side. Painted with flickering strokes of the brush, the trees grow upwards like green flaming tongues, and even the edge of the painting cannot hinder their unbridled growth; the top of the larger tree is cut off. Pure nature, growth and movement, and untamed energy are displayed – a cosmic happening perhaps? A clue to this could be the rising sickle of the moon in the star-lit night. In the summer of 1889 van Gogh wrote to Theo: "I am totally preoccupied with cypresses. I would like to create something similar to my sunflower paintings with them. I find it strange that they have never been painted in the way I see them. They are as beautifully proportioned as an Egyptian obelisk."

A much more severe attack in the autumn of 1889 took him by surprise whilst he was working on a painting done outside the asylum. Thoughts of suicide and terrible hallucinations, which only very slowly eased off, were followed by a period of deep depression. This relapse clearly reveals the chronic character of his illness. He began to fear the fellow inmates and stayed in his room; for six weeks he did not set foot

"I put my heart and soul into my work, and have half lost my mind in the process."
VINCENT VAN GOGH

The Starry Night
Saint-Rémy, June 1889
Oil on canvas, 73 × 92 cm
Metropolitan Museum of Art, New York

out of the building. Finally he began to paint again, but only inside the asylum. He wrote to his sister Willemin: "Since my illness I sense a terrible loneliness even in the open air, so that I don't dare to go outside."

This fear became evident in his choice of colour. The earlier vibrant colours of his palette gave way increasingly to toned-down colours and darker harmonies, with nothing left of the stark colour contrasts. This did not mean a return to the tonal harmony of the paintings of his Dutch period, instead this recalled the chromatic multiplicity of tone which he had discovered in Paris and Arles, and he introduced to this a series of unusual disjointed tones, which corresponded to the artist's frame of mind.

Again he uses the tree theme in the painting "Olive Orchard" (p. 70), but quite differently from the cypress paintings. Here one single movement runs through the whole of the painting's surface. Soil, trees and sky display the same wavy strokes of the brush, and so the separate unities are brought into one complete entity. The three larger areas of colour – ochre, green and blue – are more reserved and soft, the colour contrasts are also toned down. The strong lines of the branches blend in with the arabesque pattern of the softer areas of the sky, just as the blue of the sky is turned in on the leaves and stems, whose green and grey tones blend in with the soil – everything is brought into one single harmony. A calming effect is also gained by the equilibrium between cold and warm colours, establishing an almost dreamlike unreality. By using black contours the strange silhouette of the olive tree trunks, which are bent and twisted as if in pain, are marked out. A mute pain appears to pervade this nature and restlessness runs through the whole.

In Saint-Rémy van Gogh discovers true movement in his work. In his paintings from here and later from Auvers, two clearly-marked styles are seen, which are elaborated to their outmost limits – on the one hand a continuous composition of winding, wavy curves, on the other hand a complicated hatching of short, sharp dashes. Both elements are loaded with excitement and dynamic forms, clearly elements of a style of painting born out of excitement and tension.

Both linear forms are combined in his "Starry Night" (p. 71), one of his main works and at the same time one of his strangest. Once again he seized upon the theme of his night paintings from his earlier periods in Paris and Arles, but now in a totally different context. It is one of the few works which completely avoids a direct observation of nature, colours and forms come from his imagination in order to call up a particular atmosphere. A highly dramatic cosmic happening is taking place in the sky. Two gigantic spiral nebulae are entwined; eleven enormously enlarged stars with their aureoles of light break through the night; an unreal orange-coloured moon looks as if it is joined to the sun; a broad band of light – perhaps the Milky Way – is drawn across the horizon, and the deep blue sky appears to be in staggering turmoil. The immediacy and expressive powers of the painting are strengthened by the impulsive, sweeping flood of brush strokes.

Yet van Gogh does not passively yield to this exciting vision. By

Self-Portrait
Saint-Rémy, September 1889
Oil on canvas, 65 × 54 cm
Musée du Jeu de Paume, Paris

Van Gogh's Bedroom in Arles
Saint-Rémy, September 1889
Oil on canvas, 73 × 92 cm
Art Institute of Chicago, Chicago

"This time it's quite simply my bedroom –
here colour is everything; objects are
given a greater style by simplifying them,
thereby giving the impression of peace
and general sleep. Simply stated, the
picture should stir the head, or more
properly, the fantasy." VINCENT VAN GOGH

artistic means he handles this vision in a different manner in his choice of
contrasting elements to portray the happenings on this earth and so
increase the effect. The sleeping town in the forefront, which is portrayed
with short, straight strokes of the brush, contrasts to the curving shapes in
the sky; even the small yellow lights of the houses present a contrast to
the stars in their quadrangular or rectangular shape. The pointed
towering church spire – reminiscent of the north – cuts across the earth's
horizon, just like the blazing flames of the powerful cypresses: a vertical,
earthbound contrast to the circling star nebulae in the sky.

One could view this contrast as opposing powers: human striving
and effort ("reaching for the stars") against celestial, cosmic powers,
since the actual happening in the painting does not take place on earth
but in the heavens. In this picture, perhaps an apocalyptic vision, van
Gogh tries to free himself from overpowering emotions. It must also be
seen as an attempt to express pictorially his desire for the infinite in
nature.

Noon Rest (After Millet)
Saint-Rémy, January 1890
Oil on canvas, 73 × 91 cm
Musée du Jeu de Paume, Paris

Three months later, in September 1889, he painted his last self-portrait (p. 73). In this half-length picture the artist stands in a three-quarter profile against a blue-green-gray spiraled, whirling, rhythmic background. The suit, over the collarless white shirt, is almost the same colour. As a sharp contrast to this strained facial expression and the dark, fixed eyes — "a look which goes straight through one" (Antonin Artaud).

The pulsating forms of the background, the sign of excitement captured in the picture, are not determined by a set rhythm nor by a rigid pattern; they convey much more the overwhelming surge of his feelings towards his environment. Yet these emotions are held spell-bound in fixed forms and are integrated as direct chosen elements of movement in a controlled composition. In spite of all the flowing unrest, a great balance is dominant.

Towards the end of that fateful year 1889 the artist's inspiration appears to have dwindled. In the evenings he was often bored to tears in the asylum, despite the fact that he read a lot. Since he was no longer

"I have drawn into myself so much that I literally do not see any other people anymore — excepting the peasants with whom I have direct contact, since I paint them."
VINCENT VAN GOGH

75

Branches of Almond Tree in Bloom
Saint-Rémy, February 1890
Oil on canvas, 73 × 92 cm
Rijksmuseum Vincent van Gogh,
Amsterdam

"My work has gone well – the last
painting was of branches in bloom. You
will see that I painted this picture most
patiently and skilfully, in utter peace and
quiet, with the greatest certainty of brush
strokes." VINCENT VAN GOGH

able to paint in the open air, he finished copies or replicas of his own
paintings. Some of them are certainly either for his mother or his sister –
paintings such as "Van Gogh's Bedroom in Arles" (left). He had
previously taken up this motif shortly before Gauguin's arrival; this first
version was however damaged during transportation. In Saint-Rémy he
painted a copy of this from memory; it is the most brilliantly coloured of
the three versions of this theme. He himself wrote: "This time it's simply
my bedroom, only the colours should work here, and through the
simplification which gives the things a larger style, peace or complete
sleep ought to be suggested."

In spite of van Gogh's intentions the picture does not give one the
impression of total calm. The objects do not relate to one another, each
one is isolated. To add to this uneasy feeling we have in observing the
painting, all the objects have been considerably foreshortened; the floor
boards lurch steeply forward, giving the impression of almost falling
over, the window is half-open, the slanting furniture – wash table and

chairs near the bed – as well as the paintings hang over into the room. The ambivalent atmosphere lends the picture a strange, tense aura: it is the wish for cosyness, for a home, for comfort and care, which contradicts reality. Desolation, loneliness and homelessness are stronger than the desire.

In winter 1889 the number of his landscape paintings decreased; his work indoors showed a concentration on the reproduction of his earlier sketches and of sketches made by other artists. Using black-and-white lithographs, reproductions and woodcuts, which Theo had sent him from Paris, he transformed the works of Rembrandt, Delacroix and Millet into colour paintings. Above all, the monumental simplicity of Millet's peasant figures had always influenced him. Between the autumn of 1889 and spring 1890 no less than 23 mostly small paintings after Millet were painted. "You'll be amazed," he wrote to his brother in September, "how effective the 'Field Workers' [Millet] becomes through the use of colour."

This amazing effect of colour on a copy of Millet's work can best be

Cottages with Thatched Roofs
Auvers, May 1890
Oil on canvas, 72 × 91 cm
Musée du Jeu de Paume, Paris

"And I could feel a heart in all of it, the soul who had made all of it and who himself had answered the most terrible doubts with this vision, who could feel, know, understand and enjoy the highs and the lows, exterior and interior, one and all in a thousandth of a part in time – all this I could feel when I write the words . . ."
HUGO VON HOFMANNSTHAL, letter of 26th May 1901

77

seen in the "Noon Rest" (p. 75). Almost two thirds of the painting is taken up by the gold-yellow-orange of the cut, tied and stacked hay. A strong contrast in colour to this is the light blue of the sky, which is echoed in the blue clothing of the peasants sleeping in the shade. Stretched out, they are after protection from the blazing midday heat, and in their sleep appear to be at one with nature. Earth and sky, man and nature form one single unit belonging together.

The most intensive, radiant and clearest blue sky that van Gogh ever painted can be seen in the background of the painting "Branches of Almond Tree in Bloom" (p. 76), which was thought of as a christening present for his little nephew, who was born at the end of January 1890 and who received his uncle's name, Vincent. The glowing white almond blossoms break forth from the still-wintery branches and, heralding spring, they proclaim the beginning of a new life. In this painting Vincent practised patience and self-discipline, which was something totally alien to his work. He perhaps restrained himself too much since during his work on this painting, his last from Saint-Rémy, he became ill.

In January and February 1890 more exciting things than the birth of his nephew and his being called after Vincent happened: for the first time an extensive article was written about him in an art magazine. The exhibition of the Brussels group "Les XX" was opened in Paris, where van Gogh showed a few of his paintings; at the same time, the new exhibition of the "Independents" was being prepared for March, in which he was also to take part. Finally he received the news of the sale of his painting "Red Vineyard" in Brussels for 400 francs to Anna Boch, the sister of the poet Eugène Boch. It was one of the few paintings which Vincent was able to sell during his life time, though not, as rumour has it, the only one.

The events of the last weeks proved too much for him. He suffered a new attack, which lasted longer than the other ones, almost two months. Again he suffered from derangement, fear of death and shocks, accompanied by hallucinations and fits of rage. Only after several weeks had gone by did he venture to write. Vincent had decided once and for all to leave the asylum. After making a short trip to Paris to visit his brother and family he travelled in May 1890 to Auvers-sur-Oise near Paris, where the doctor and hobby painter Dr. Gachet had agreed to look after Vincent. He rented a room in the Ravoux Inn opposite the small town hall, and immediately began to paint again, making use of the new motifs which the place and surroundings offered him. The painting "Cottages with Thatched Roofs" (p. 77) is a witness to his renewed vital creativity, although it appears to have been painted more fleetingly than ever. A lot of things in the painting are only vaguely shown, open forms and contours and loose strokes of the brush lead one to conclude that the painting was done in a hurry. Despite the idyllic motif of the old, thatched roofs of the farm houses with vegetable garden, fence and wall, a great unrest is spread over the whole of the painting by the bushes and dark trees.

A nervous energy appears to have taken hold of the artist again. The

Road with Man Walking, Carriage, Cypress, Star and Crescent Moon
Saint-Rémy, May 1890
Oil on canvas, 92 × 73 cm
Rijksmuseum Kröller-Müller, Otterlo

In this way the real landscape takes on an almost celestial character, also called up by the central ordering of the dark cypresses, which dominate the whole picture, placed between sun and moon with their wide halos of light. Two fully grown trees intertwining with one another try with all their might to reach upwards. The ground is full of similar forms, with the yellow field, the sloping stream of the road and the flat blue range of mountains in the background, which are reflected in the green blades of grass on the edge of the road. As a stark contrast to all this movement are the two figures on the road, the horse pulling the yellow carriage and the house lit up on the right-hand side of the picture. In each area the brush strokes take on a special character: concentrated in the sky, parallel, interweaving and converging on the ground, flame-like tongues of the intertwining trees extending upwards. Everything in the picture is transformed into a pulsating rigidity.

During these weeks it was only due to his work that van Gogh could forget about his illness. Painting was not only a therapy for him, it was his whole life. During the seventy days he spent in Auvers, he painted as if possessed. More than eighty pictures arose from the period, amongst which is the masterpiece "The Church in Auvers" (repr. p. 62). The exactly defined form of the church gives the impression of it being a compact sculpture, which forms an organic unit with nature. The cobalt-blue sky is a colour of the night, the whole scene appears dark and the light unreal. A similar darker sky with the same effect of light appears in the later works "Wheat Field with Crows", with the v-shaped division in the forefront, which gives the impression of wider space.

Already in Saint-Rémy he had often been preoccupied with religious thoughts and he had also painted some biblical themes. His own religious sincerity forbade him to create biblical figures from his own fantasy; he did not dare to do this, and thus he looked to the old masters for his models. The choice of themes alone reveals the motif for his religious paintings: he depicted the dead Christ in the arms of his mother, the raising of Lazarus, to whom he gave his own features, the good Samaritan – suffering figures, who hope for future redemption.

"The Good Samaritan" (right) was modelled on Delacroix' "Pietà". linear parts of the painting are stressed and maintain the lead over the dark, earth-colour palette. This becomes clear in the painting "Road with Man Walking, Carriage, Cypress, Star, and Crescent Moon" (right). The distinct brush strokes, so marked in all of van Gogh's works, now become a true torrent, an avalanche, which pours over the whole of the canvas. Now the actual brush strokes take prominence just as the colours did in Arles. Objects have lost their stable form, their outlines have been extended lengthways, wind about and coil in on themselves. These connect the motif, consisting of many tiny streaming parts which follow the movement of the outline. Their colours are disjointed and dull – the colour energy is transferred to the lines of energy. These lines of energy appear as different centres of power, penetrating and struggling for dominance of place like magnetic fields which both draw and repel one another.

The Good Samaritan (After Delacroix)
Saint-Rémy, May 1890
Oil on canvas, 73 × 60 cm
Rijksmuseum Kröller-Müller, Otterlo

Delacroix, like Millet, was both his patron-saint of art and the founder of colour techniques. The reticent wealth of colour in this picture is meant to remind one of his great master. The brighter colours, the characteristic blue and red of Delacroix, are placed in an environment of more neutral, brownish colour tones, which are cleverly connected to one another in graded intervals of warm and cold, light and dark tones. Van Gogh adds a stream of parallel brush strokes to Delacroix' original rhythm in his dynamic sketch. The arabesque forms and winding curves of the Delacroix painting are transferred by van Gogh into disjointed linear strokes – a devoted "translation" of the old work into a "modern" pictorial language.

But most of all, even more so than the religious pictures and landscapes, van Gogh was occupied with portrait painting – that is, the modern portrait. His models were always the simple, plain people around him. It was not for an external beauty or a certain character trait that he painted these people, but because of their mere humanity. Although brought to the front of the painting, they still have something mysterious and unusual about them. The smooth loveliness of his previous portrait paintings was now totally given up. The face now took on a landscape-like appearance, due to the coarse texture of the paint, and the skin took on a tougher, yet natural constitution.

The composition "Peasant Woman with Straw Hat" (right) is typical of this. The three-quarter length figure of the young peasant girl sits somewhat stiffly and bashful amongst the high sheafs of corn, her cheeks glowing in the same red as the poppies. The pure blue of her blouse, inlaid with tiny orange spots, contrasts with the warm tones of the corn and her apron, as well as the golden yellow of her hat and the orange-coloured shadow cast by it. Once again one can see traces of the realism and coarseness of his earlier brown-toned peasant pictures.

In spite of this, this portrait remains in the shadow of his uncontested masterpiece of portrait painting – his "Portrait of Dr. Gachet" (p. 85). This strange eccentric personality, who himself was a painter and friends with a lot of Impressionist painters, had deeply influenced van Gogh. Melancholy, sadness and resignation, which can be read in Gachet's face – a "despairing expression of our time" – pervade and set the tone of the whole painting. All lines and colours are adapted to this melancholy atmosphere and form an original unity. Mainly the lines follow the depressive tendency of the figure, betraying the mood of this sensitive, simple man. The background lines correspond to those of the cap, face and shoulders. Thanks to the ultramarine blue of his jacket, the figure's face is highlighted and becomes paler at the same time. His woeful, pale-blue eyes gaze into the distant. A continuum of pale to dark blue – in the sky, background hills and suit – dominates the whole picture and is to be found again in the flower and the doctor's pupils.

The foundation was laid for a great friendship between the two men, not least because of this portrait. Gachet liked it so much that he asked van Gogh to paint a second version of the portrait. Art was a strong bond in their friendship and van Gogh was overjoyed to be able, at long last, to

Peasant Woman with Straw Hat
Auvers, June 1890
Oil on canvas, 92 × 73 cm
H. R. Hahnloser collection, Berne

Portrait of Dr. Gachet with Pipe
Auvers, June 1890
Etching, 18 × 15 cm
Rijksprentenkabinet, Amsterdam

"Mr Gachet seems to me to be just as ill and as nervous as you and I, as well as being much older. He lost his wife a few years ago. But he's a doctor, nevertheless, that's what keeps him going – this manual skill and belief. We're quite good friends already. I'm working on his portrait – his head is covered by a white cap; his blond hair I've painted in really light tones; the colour of the skin on his hands is also really fair; a blue jacket; the background a cobalt blue. He props himself up against a red table on which a yellow book and foxglove with purplish flowers stand."

VINCENT VAN GOGH

**Portrait of Dr. Gachet Seated
at a Table**
Auvers, June 1890
Oil on canvas, 66 × 57 cm
S. Kramarsky Trust Fund, New York

paint someone who really understood his work. After such a long period of loneliness he had finally found a person with whom he could discuss his paintings.

Yet Vincent's artistic happiness was not to be long-lived. Things were not going well for his beloved brother Theo, whose financial and moral support Vincent needed to be able to survive. Theo's child was seriously ill, his wife was totally exhausted from endless sleepless nights, and often disputes arose between himself and the gallery owners, who no longer had faith in his artistic judgement. Greatly worried about his brother, Vincent travelled to Paris in July. Theo's difficulties also threatened his own existence, and thus his nerves began to suffer. He did not stay the whole length of his time there. From Auvers he wrote to Theo: "After my return here I am still very sad and the misfortunes, which are threatening you, lie heavy on my heart . . . my very steps are uncertain. I am afraid I'm a great burden to you, since I'm living from your financial help."

On top of this he also fell out with Gachet. He even told his brother about it: "In my opinion I don't think we can rely on Dr. Gachet at all. I get the impression that he is more ill than myself, or let's say at least just as ill. If a blind man leads the blind, don't they then both fall by the wayside?" This disagreement with Gachet must have deeply upset him. Even here in his new surroundings, complete and utter loneliness threatened him again. Yet he did not in any way attempt to avoid this threatening loneliness. He worked all the more on his own, since Gachet had completely stopped all his visits and invitations.

His work was the only thing which kept him alive. Often he painted to near exhaustion, every day a new painting, sometimes even two. One month before his death he painted "The Wheat Field with Crows" (pp. 86/87), which clearly echoed his mood during those days. In this painting he attempted to convey his "sadness and extreme loneliness". The expanse of the field is conveyed by the unusually wide format of the picture, which opens up into three separating ways at the front. The observer is unsettled by not knowing where both the horizon and the path end, in the field or off the edge of the painting somewhere. The normal structural perspective of the wide open fields is turned upside down – its lines of alignment run from the horizon to meet in the front of the painting. The space presented here has no perspectual centre to it any more. The blue sky and the yellow fields push forcibly away from one another, and a flock of crows crosses the boundaries to the uncertain forefront.

In contrast to his turbulent paintings, the whole space in this painting is filled with a succinct breadth and simplicity. The colour palette is reduced entirely to the three basic colours and one complementary colour – the blue of the sky, the complementary yellow of the corn, the red of the separating paths and the complementary green of the blades of grass along these paths – and thus creates an overall image of control. The predominant horizontal line is determined from the artist's state of mind rather than from the frame or canvas. It presents

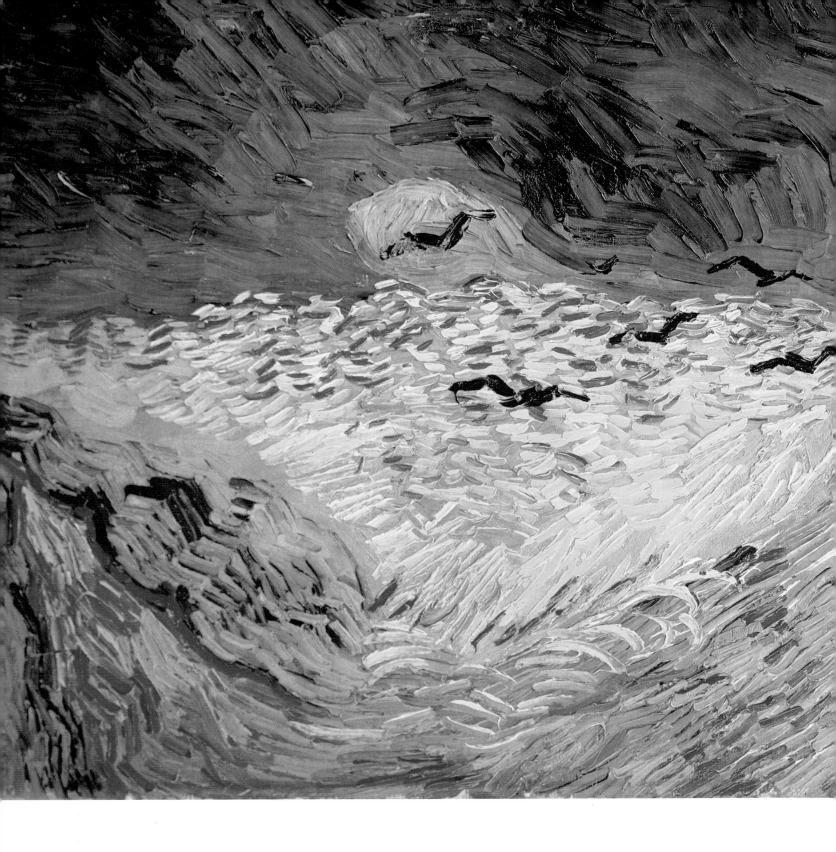

neither a panorama, nor is it created by the things that dominate the space, so that there are barely any vertical values. In all, parts and wholes, closeness and distance cannot be definitely distinguished from one another.

Indeed one could almost say that because of this absolutely valid formulation of the theme of a landscape, which appears to reflect the original laws of creation, many believe this picture to be one of his last. Yet a dozen more followed, amongst others the "Cottages at Chaponval"

"I experience a period of frightening clarity in those moments when nature is so beautiful. I am no longer sure of myself, and the paintings appear as in a dream." VINCENT VAN GOGH

86

(p. 89). Yet the power and quality of the "Cornfield Painting" is never attained again. So it is quite valid to say that this painting is one of the most complete testimonies to his art form.

Vincent's last, unfinished letter to Theo on 27th July 1890 sounds like a farewell: "I would really like to write to you about a lot of things, yet I feel this is useless . . . In my own work I put my whole life in jeopardy, and I have half lost my mind in the process . . . I repeat to you again that I have always looked upon you as something different than an

Wheat Field with Crows
Auvers, July 1890
Oil on canvas, 50,5 × 100,5 cm
Rijksmuseum Vincent van Gogh,
Amsterdam

87

> "Everywhere the sky is a wonderful blue, the sun is a pale sulphurous yellow, and this is as good and as charming as the juxtaposition of sky blue and yellow in Johannes Vermeer's paintings. I can't paint as beautifully as him, but I become so immersed in the very act of painting, that I forget and let myself go, without paying heed to any rules whatsoever."
>
> VINCENT VAN GOGH

Village Street in Auvers
Auvers, July 1890
Oil on canvas, 73 × 92 cm
Ateneumin Taidemuseo, Helsinki

ordinary art dealer . . ." One could even say that without his brother, who supported him all his life, Vincent would not have had the means to paint such pictures.

Yet now his life support was himself in great difficulty, and thus Vincent's further existence was put into question. The catastrophe appeared unavoidable. His relationship with Gachet had come to a final end. All his contacts to his environment were destroyed and with this the hope of work, which had up until now kept him alive. In the end the continually recurring attacks sounded the alarm for his final madness.

His situation was hopeless – van Gogh had failed totally in life. Yet one way still remained. On the evening of 27th July 1890 he went at dusk into the fields and shot himself in the chest with a revolver. With all his strength he managed to drag himself back to the inn; here he died two days later in the arms of his brother, who had hurried to his side.

This marked the end of the singular life of an artist who defies comparison with any other. In his art, which he had arduously wrestled with and which he finally paid for with his life, van Gogh dared a

synthesis such as hardly any contemporary artist has dared since. Art and life became an inseparable unit to him, and with this he realized an ancient artistic dream of reality. To create works of art meant no less to him than to paint life, not mere reality, but the principle of life.

Van Gogh had not only developed the three fundamental elements of painting – colour, line and composition – into further artistic elements of style, but also endowed them with a new and unique significance: colours as the breath of life, which grants all things life; the line as a principal of movement, as the dynamics of life and as indestructible energy; the composition as a place of feelings for his view of the world. Fulfillment and loneliness, desire and doubt, love and destruction, devotion and flight from reality, closeness and distance, duration and transistoriness – all these things, one person, an artist, painted in his work. He sought consolation in his art from the world and life which he loved, but whose love was not returned. He suffered in this world and was destroyed by it. With his art he created his own new world, which was full of colour and movement and contained everything he knew about existence.

Cottages at Chaponval
Auvers, July 1890
Oil on canvas, 65 × 81 cm
Kunsthaus, Zurich

"I can't change the fact that my paintings don't sell. But the time will come when people will recognize that they are worth more than the value of the paints used in the picture." VINCENT VAN GOGH

Vincent van Gogh 1853–1890: Life and Works

1853   Vincent Willem van Gogh, born on 30th March in the Dutch village vicarage of Groot-Zundert (North Brabant), the first of six children to Theodorus van Gogh (1822–1885), a preacher in the Dutch Reformed Church, and his wife Anne Cornelia, née Carbentus (1819–1907), the daughter of a bookbinder from The Hague. He is named after the still-born child who died on this very day the previous year.

1857   Birth of his brother Theodorus, called Theo.

1861–1864   Attends the village school in Zundert.

1864   Enrolls in the private boarding-school in Zevenbergen. Learns French, English and German, practises drawing.

1866–1868   Attends the boarding-school in Tilburg.

1868   Gives up school and goes back to Groot-Zundert.

1869   Goes to The Hague where he enters the branch office of the Paris art dealer Goupil & Cie, founded originally by his uncle Vincent. Under the supervision of H. G. Tersteeg he sells reproductions of works of art; reads extensively and visits museums.

1871   His father is translated as a vicar to Helvoirt in Brabant where he moves with his family.

1872   Spends his holidays at his parents' and then visits his brother in The Hague. This marks the beginning of the extensive exchange of letters between them.

1873   JANUARY: Is transferred on the initiative of his uncle to the Brussels branch of Goupil.
MAY: Transfer to the London branch. Before his departure he travels to Paris, which impresses him deeply; visits the Louvre.
JUNE: Works for a year with Goupil in London. On his walks he makes his first sketches, which he throws away. Falls in love with Ursula, the daughter of his landlady. Her rejection of his love precipitates a personal crisis in him. NOVEMBER: His brother Theo is transferred to the Goupil branch in The Hague.

1874   SUMMER: Spends his holidays with his parents in Helvoirt and confides in them his private disappointment to explain his depressive mood. Goes back to London together with his sister Anna in the middle of July. Leads a lonely life and shows little interest in his work; reads a lot, especially religious writings. OCTOBER–DECEMBER: His uncle makes him transfer temporarily to the main office of Goupil in Paris; this change of environment was hoped to improve his situation.

1875   MAY: Final transfer to Paris. Continues to neglect his work, much to the annoyance of his colleagues and clients alike; visits museums and galleries, is enthusiastic about Corot and the 17th century Dutch School of painting.

Vincent's brother Theo, around 1888–1890.

Vincent at the age of 13 in the year 1866. This picture was probably taken after he finished boarding-school in Zevenbergen and before he entered the secondary school in Tilburg.

Vincent's father Theodorus van Gogh. Drawing by Vincent van Gogh, Etten, July 1881. Pen-and-ink, washed, 33 × 25 cm. Private ownership, The Hague.

OCTOBER: Father Theodorus is translated to Etten, near Breda.
DECEMBER: Without having applied for leave beforehand, he spends Christmas with his parents.

1876   APRIL: Hands in his notice at Goupil's. Goes to Ramsgate, near London, and works as a supply teacher, receiving only board and lodgings.
JULY–DECEMBER: Continues to work as a supply teacher in Isleworth, a working-class area on the outskirts of London. Afterwards he works as an apprentice lay preacher and teacher together with a Methodist preacher. In November he preaches his first sermon; wants to devote his life to the evangelization of the poor people. In his spare time he still continues his interest in painting; visits the gallery in Hampton Court. At Christmas he visits his parents in Etten; worried about their son's condition, they prevent his return to London.

1877   JANUARY–APRIL: On his uncle's recommendation he gets a position as an assistant in a bookshop in Dordrecht. Leads a very lonely life, frequently visits the church and translates parts of the Bible into various languages; also draws.
MAY: Convinces his father of his religious vocation. Goes to Amsterdam in order to prepare himself for the entrance examination at the Theological Faculty. Lives with his uncle Johannes, head of the municipal dockyards. Takes lessons in Latin, Greek and mathematics. Reads extensively, visits museums and draws. His studies prove extremely difficult and in the end he gives up.

1878   JULY: Returns home and then goes with his father to Brussels. There he intends to do a three-month course in preaching in order to become a lay preacher. As the course doesn't begin until August he goes back to Etten.

Vincent around 1872.

AUGUST–OCTOBER: Attends the Evangelist school in Laeken, near Brussels, but is considered unsuitable for the lay-preaching profession. So he returns to Etten.
DECEMBER: Tries to follow his vocation and travels to the Borinage, the Belgian coal mining area close to the French border. Lives in extreme poverty, visits sick people and reads the Bible to the miners.

1879   JANUARY–JULY: Permission to work for six months as a lay preacher in Wasmes in the Borinage. Lives in a hut and sleeps on straw. Is deeply concerned about the living conditions of the miners, whom he supports with all his might. His envolvement in the plight of the poor irritates his superiors, who do not extend his contract under the pretext that his rhetorical talents are insufficient.
AUGUST: Walks to Brussels to get advice from vicar Pieterson. Shows him his sketches of the miners in the Borinage.

Returns to the coal-mining area of Cuesmes where he follows his vocation at his own discretion and without any payment. Stays there until July 1880. Supports the poor and sick people although he himself is living in extreme poverty. Reads a lot – Dickens, Hugo, Shakespeare – continues to draw and becomes more and more interested in painting. Experiences a period of deep personal crisis which is to mould his later life. Stops writing to his brother Theo for a while due to the latter's criticism of his choice of profession.

1880   JULY: Writes to Theo again, who supports him financially. Theo now works at Goupil's in Paris. Vincent describes his state of agonizing uncertainty.
AUGUST–SEPTEMBER: Avidly makes sketches of the miners' environment; Theo encourages him. Copies works by Millet.
OCTOBER: Goes to Brussels where he studies anatomical and perspective drawing at the Academy of Art. Admires Millet and Daumier. In November he makes the acquaintance of the Dutch painter Rappard; they become friends. Stays in Brussels until April 1881.

1881   SPRING: Meets Theo in Etten to discuss his artistic future. Does not return to Brussels. Draws landscapes. Goes on hikes with Rappard who visits him.
SUMMER: Sadly for him he falls in love with his cousin Kate (Kee) Vos-Stricker; she has just become a widow and is visiting his family in Etten with her child. Kee returns early to Amsterdam. Vincent travels to The Hague and visits the painter Mauve, whom he admires greatly.
AUTUMN: Goes to Amsterdam with the intention of marrying Kee, but she does not even receive him. To bear out his firm conviction he holds his hand in the flame of a lamp while his parents watch.
NOVEMBER–DECEMBER: Visits Mauve in The

Presbytery (in the middle) in Groot-Zundert, birthplace of Vincent and Theo van Gogh. Vincent was born in the little attic room with the flag.

View into the interior of The Hague branch office of the art dealer Goupil & Cie. Here Vincent was introduced into the art trade.

View of the vicarage in Nuenen.

Vincent's lover Clasina Maria Hoornik sat as a model for this drawing. "Sorrow". Black chalk, 44,5 × 27 cm. The Hague, April 1882. Garman Ryan collection, London.

Hague and there he paints, for the first time, still lifes in oils and watercolours. His relationship with his parents deteriorates mainly due to Vincent's refusal to give up Kee and because of his advocation of extreme religious views. He quarrels with his father at Christmas. Vincent refuses to accept money from his father and leaves Etten.

1882 JANUARY: Vincent moves to The Hague and lives in the same area as Mauve, who teaches him the techniques of painting and also lends him some money. Theo sends him 100 to 200 florins every month. His relationship with Mauve deteriorates because of Vincent's refusal to work from plaster models. Gets to know Clasina Maria Hoornik, called Sien, a prostitute and an alcoholic. Sien is pregnant and Vincent takes care of her. She serves as his model.

MARCH: Severs ties with Mauve, whom he still admires. His relationships to the other painters become strained. Only Weissenbuch appreciates his work. Bases a lot of his drawings on nature; finds his models, except Sien, in the slums; his only commission comes from his uncle Cornelius who orders twenty pen-and-ink drawings of the city.
JUNE: Is cured of gonorrhoea in the local

hospital. His father and Tersteeg visit him. Wants to marry Sien in spite of the opposition of his family and friends. Takes her to Leiden where she can give birth to her child; looks for a flat for the future family.
SUMMER: Concerns himself with the various uses and techniques of colour, in order to prepare himself for his later paintings using oils. Theo gives him some money for painting material. Paints mainly landscapes (see p. 9). Father accepts a position as a vicar in Nuenen, where he moves with his family.
AUTUMN: Stays in The Hague until the summer of 1883. Paints landscapes and draws scenes from nature. In the winter he makes sketches and draws portraits; his

models are ordinary people, inhabitants of old people's homes and Sien with the new-born child. Gets to know the painter Weele, with whom he paints in the dunes next spring. Begins to take an interest in lithography. Continues to read a lot, even journals like "Harper's Weekly" and "The Graphic".

1883 SEPTEMBER–NOVEMBER: As a result of talks with Theo his painful decision to separate from Sien with whom he has lived together for a year. Goes alone to Drente, a province in the north. Travels by boat to Nieuw-Amsterdam; there he goes on long walks. The landscape with its dark peat bogs fascinates him as it has fascinated Liebermann and his friends Mauve, Rappard and Weele before him. Draws and paints the hard working peasants of that region. Visits the old village of Zweeloo where Liebermann lived for a long time.
DECEMBER: Moves to Nuenen, the home of his parents. There he stays until November 1885. Paints about 200 pictures during these two years, which are characterized by a dark and earthy tonality. Besides Zola he reads theoretical texts on art by Delacroix and Fromentin and he is convinced of the close relationship between colour and music (Wagner); takes singing and piano lessons. His parents want to help Vincent; overlooking his eccentric clothing and strange behaviour, he is allowed to make a studio in a side building adjoining the vicarage.

1884 JANUARY: His mother breaks a leg and has to stay in bed for a long time; Vincent takes loving care of her.
MAY: Moves his studio into the house of the Catholic sacristan. Rappard pays him a visit.
AUGUST: Both sets of parents fight against his brief love-affair with Margot Begemann, a neighbour. Margot attempts suicide.
AUGUST–SEPTEMBER: Paints six decorative pictures for the dining-room of the goldsmith Hermans in Eindhoven.

Vincent works as a lay preacher in the Borinage, the coal-mining area on the Belgian-French border. The picture shows the Nr. 7 mine in Wasmes.

The Rue Lepic on Montmartre, Paris. In June 1886 Theo van Gogh moved into house Nr. 54 where he accommodated his brother, whom he allows to make a studio there.

Paris: "The Hill of Montmartre with Windmills".
Paris winter 1886.
Oil on canvas, 36 × 61 cm.
Rijksmuseum Kröller-Müller, Otterlo.

Paris: "The Moulin de la Galette".
Paris, summer 1886.
Oil on canvas, 38,5 × 46 cm.
Rijksmuseum Kröller-Müller, Otterlo.

OCTOBER: Rappard visits him in Nuenen.
OCTOBER–NOVEMBER: Gives some amateurs painting lessons in Eindhoven; together they go on walks and visit museums.
DECEMBER: In the winter he is busy sketching portraits; before this, peasants and weavers at work and landscapes were his main themes.

1885 On the 26th March his father Theodorus dies of a stroke. Vincent is heart-broken. After a quarrel with his sister Anna he moves into the studio in the house of the sacristan.
APRIL–MAY: Paints "The Potato Eaters" (p. 14), the main work of his Dutch period. Sends a lithograph of the motif to Rappard who criticizes it and in so doing precipitates the end of their friendship.
SEPTEMBER: The Catholic priest forbids the villagers to sit as models for him (since a peasant woman, whom he had drawn before, had become pregnant). Draws still lives of potatoes and bird's nests.
OCTOBER: Travels with his friend Kerssemakers from Eindhoven to Amsterdam and visits the Rijksmuseum. Rembrandt and Hals fascinate him.
NOVEMBER: At the end of the month he moves to Antwerp where he stays until February 1886. Wants to get in touch with artists and tries to sell his pictures. Visits museums and is above all impressed by Rubens. While scouting through the city he discovers some Japanese woodcuts, which he then buys.

1886 JANUARY: Enrols at the Ecole des Beaux-Arts; takes courses in painting and drawing. His disapproval of the academic method of teaching here leads to disagreements. But nevertheless he takes part in the entrance examination for the senior classes.

FEBRUARY: Is sick for a month due to malnutrition, overwork and heavy smoking. At the end of February he comes to Paris in order to take lessons from Cormon.
MARCH: Arrives in Paris and arranges a meeting with Theo at the Louvre. Theo, who runs a small gallery for Goupil at the Boulevard Montmartre, accommodates him. In the meantime the academy in Antwerp rejects his specimens and demotes him to the beginners' course.
APRIL–MAY: Studies in the studio of Cormon where he makes the acquaintance of Bernard, Russel and Toulouse-Lautrec. Theo also introduces him to Monet, Renoir, Sisley, Pissarro, Degas, Signac and Seurat. From now on the colours on his palette become considerably brighter, noticeable in his still lifes and flower paintings.
MAY: His mother leaves Nuenen. A second-hand dealer buys up all the pictures he left in the house, sells them off for ten centimes each and burns the unsold rest.
JUNE: Moves with Theo to the Rue Lepic on Montmartre where he is allowed to

Vincent (with his back to the camera) with his friend Emile Bernard on the banks of the Seine in Asnières, 1886.

establish a studio. Paints Paris city views in the style of the Pointillists.
WINTER: Makes friends with Gauguin, who comes from Pont-Aven to Paris. Due to Vincent's difficult character his relationship to Theo, who is suffering from a nervous disease, becomes more and more strained. Vincent writes to his sister and tells her that life with Theo is "almost unbearable".

1887 SPRING: Meets Bernard in "Père" Tanguy's paint shop. Both of them work in Asnières, on the banks of the Seine. In discussions with Bernard and Gauguin Vincent refuses to consider Impressionism as a final stage in the development of painting. Buys Japanese woodcuts in the "Bing" gallery. Frequently visits the "Café de Tambourin" on the Boulevard de Clichy; brief love-affair with the owner Agostina Segatori (see p. 21), a former model of Corot and Degas. There he exhibits together with Bernard, Gauguin and Toulouse-Lautrec and he decorates the walls with Japanese coloured woodcuts. This group is called "Peintres du Petit Boulevard" in contrast to the "Peintres du Grand Boulevard" (Monet, Sisley, Pissarro, Degas, Seurat), who exhibit in Theo's gallery.
SUMMER: Paints several pictures using the techniques of Pointillism.

1888 FEBRUARY: Vincent leaves Paris where he has painted more than 200 pictures during the last two years and goes to Arles. He is attracted by the bright light of the south and by the warmth of the colours. Presumably Toulouse-Lautrec has influenced this decision.
MARCH: Dreams of living together in an artists' commune which would eliminate all material needs. Paints many pictures with blooming flowers and trees which

Self-portrait (Noon: Rest).
Arles, September 1888.
Oil on canvas, 62 × 52 cm.
Fogg Art Museum, Harvard University, Cambridge
(Mass.)

Superintendent of the mental hospital in Saint-Rémy.
Saint-Rémy, September 1889.
Oil on canvas, 61 × 46 cm.
Dübi-Müller collection, Solothurn.

Self-portrait.
Saint-Rémy, September 1889.
Oil on canvas, 57 × 43,5 cm.
John Hay Whitney collection, New York.

remind him of Japanese landscapes. On receiving the news of Mauve's death he dedicates a picture to his memory (see p. 35). At the Paris "Salon des Artistes Indépendants" three of his pictures are exhibited.

MAY: Rents for 15 francs a month the right wing, consisting of four rooms, of the "yellow house" on Place Lamartine; here he wants to realize his dream of the artists' commune. Until the flat is furnished he sleeps at the "Café de Alcazar" (see pp. 44/45) and takes his meals in the station restaurant of Madame Ginoux (p. 51). Paints the famous "Drawbridge with Lady with Parasol" (p. 33).
JUNE: After a trip to Saintes-Marie-de-la-Mer he paints pictures with boats (p. 37). Gets to know the second lieutenant of the Zouaves Milliet (p. 39), who takes painting lessons from him and accompanies Vincent on walks.

JULY: Many landscapes paintings are made during the numerous outings to Montmajour near Arles (see p. 36). Stimulated by the reading of Loti's "Madame Chrysanthème" he paints the portrait "Mousmé, Sitting in a Cane Chair" (p. 40).

AUGUST: Makes friends with the country postman Joseph Roulin, whose portrait he paints (pp. 42 and 43). Sends his brother Theo 35 pictures via the Zouave Milliet. Paints a series of sunflowers (see p. 30).
SEPTEMBER: More and more he paints out of doors at night. Whilst doing so he fixes candles to the brim of his hat and to the easel (see p. 47). Gets to know the Belgian

poet and painter Boch and makes friends with him. Moves into the "yellow house".
OCTOBER: After Vincent's repeated requests Gauguin finally comes to Arles. The two live and work together.
DECEMBER: Visits together with Gauguin the museum in Montpellier where they see Courbet's painting "Bonjour, Monsieur Courbet", which was Gauguin's inspiration for a later picture. Disputes arise between them, described later by Vincent as "exaggerated tensions". After having lived together for two months their relationship begins to deteriorate. According to Gauguin's report, Vincent attacks him with a razor blade on 23rd December. Gauguin rushes out of the house and spends the night in an inn. During this night Vincent suffers a fit of mental derangement and cuts off the lower part of his left ear. He wraps it in newspaper and takes it as a present to the prostitute Rachel in the brothel. The next morning the police find him lying injured

The "Alcazar" in Arles, where Vincent paints his famous "Night Café" (p. 44/45).

The hotel and restaurant Carrel in Rue Cavalerie 30, Vincent's first lodgings in Arles.

"The yellow house" in Arles (see p. 48). Vincent rented the right wing.

Van Gogh's room in the mental hospital Saint-Paul-de-Mausole in Saint-Rémy, with an iron bed and chair.

25ᵐᵉ ANNÉE N° 53   CINQ CENTIMES LE NUMÉRO   30 DÉCEMBRE 1888

LE FORUM RÉPUBLICAIN
JOURNAL DE L'ARRONDISSEMENT D'ARLES
Paraissant tous les Dimanches

Chronique locale

— Dimanche dernier, à 11 heures 1|2 du soir, le nommé Vincent Vaugogh, peintre, originaire de Hollande, s'est présenté à la maison de tolérance n° 1, a demandé la nommée Rachel, et lui a remis ... son oreille en lui disant : « Gardez cet objet précieusement. » Puis il a disparu. Informée de ce fait qui ne pouvait être que celui d'un pauvre aliéné, la police s'est rendue le lendemain matin chez cet individu qu'elle a trouvé couché dans son lit, ne donnant presque plus signe de vie.

Ce malheureux a été admis d'urgence à l'hospice.

The "Forum Républicain" of 30ᵗʰ December, with the report on Vincent's cut ear.

The Ravoux Inn in Auvers where Vincent lived in 1890.

in his bed and take him to hospital. Gauguin leaves and informs Theo about his brother's condition. Immediately Theo comes to Arles. Epilepsy, dipsomania and schizophrenia are the presumed causes of his illness.

1889 JANUARY: From the hospital Vincent writes a letter to Theo (see p. 61) and tells him that he is feeling better; he adds some cordial words for Gauguin. On the 7ᵗʰ he moves into the "yellow house". Writes reassuring letters to his mother and sister although he suffers from sleeplessness. Paints two self-portraits showing his bandaged ear (p. 59).
FEBRUARY: Because of sleeplessness and recurring hallucinations he has to go back into hospital; in between his hospital stays he again and again paints in the "yellow house".
MARCH: On account of a petition, instigated by the citizens of Arles, Vincent has to be brought back into hospital.
APRIL: Signac visits him; they are allowed to go back into his house, which in the meantime has been closed by the police. Theo marries Johanna Bogner, the sister of a friend. Vincent paints again and sends Theo two boxes full of masterpieces.
MAY: Although he feels better he goes of his own accord into the mental hospital Saint-Paul-de-Mausole near Saint-Rémy-de-Provence. Theo pays for two rooms for him, one as a studio with a view of the garden. Is allowed to paint outdoors

Van Gogh's death chamber in the Ravoux Inn in Auvers.

under the supervision of the ward attendant Poulet; paints mainly landscapes.
JUNE: At the end of the month he paints cypresses (pp. 65, 67, 69, 70 and 71).
JULY: After a visit to Arles he suffers a severe attack whilst painting outdoors. Is unconscious for a time and his memory is impaired.
AUGUST–NOVEMBER: Continues to paint, but with interruptions. Copies Millet and Delacroix liberally. Writes to Theo and tells him that he wants to come back to the north. Sends six pictures to Brussels to be exhibited at the "Les XX" show.
DECEMBER: Sends Theo three parcels with pictures. During another attack he attempts to swallow paint.

1890 JANUARY: Has an exhibition in Brussels. Toulouse-Lautrec challenges a painter who criticizes Vincent's pictures to a duel. First enthusiastic criticism in the "Mercure de France". Writes to Theo telling him that he has never felt more at peace. On the 31ˢᵗ Theo's son is born and baptized Vincent Willem after his uncle and godfather.
FEBRUARY: Dedicates the "Branches of an Almond Tree in Blossom" (p. 76) to his nephew. Theo informs him that Anne Boch has bought his picture "Red Vineyard" for 400 francs in Brussels. Immediately afterwards he suffers another heavy attack which forces him to rest for more than a month. Exhibits ten paintings at the Paris "Salon des Artistes Indépendants".
MAY: After his latest crisis he visits Theo and his family in Paris. He then settles in Auvers-sur-Oise, near Paris. For the time being he lives in the Saint Aubin inn, then in the café owned by the Ravoux couple. Theo has chosen Auvers because Dr. Gachet, himself a hobby painter and friend of the Impressionists, is living here and he agrees to take care of Vincent.

Gachet admires Vincent's art and they become friends. In Auvers he paints more than eighty pictures.
JUNE: Spends a weekend at Gachet's house together with his brother's family. Paints "The Church in Auvers" (p. 62).
JULY: Visits Theo in Paris where he also meets Toulouse-Lautrec. Due to Theo's professional worries and the ill-health of his son, Vincent soon returns to Auvers. Paints several pictures of a larger format showing fields under a thunderstorm sky (pp. 86/87). On the 23ʳᵈ he writes his last letter. On the afternoon of the 27ᵗʰ he goes out, comes home late and retires to his room. Mr. and Mrs. Ravoux notice that he is suffering great pain. Vincent confesses that he has shot a bullet into his breast. Gachet dresses his wounds and informs Theo. On the 29ᵗʰ he sits the whole day in his bed smoking a pipe. He dies in the night and is buried at the cemetery of Auvers on the following day. Besides Theo and Gachet some friends from Paris, amongst them Bernard and "Père" Tanguy, take part in the funeral.

1891 After Vincent's death Theo's sorrow increases. He dies on the 25ᵗʰ January in Utrecht. In 1914 his corpse is exhumed and buried next to Vincent's grave in Auvers.

The gravestones of Vincent and Theo at the cemetery in Auvers.

The following titles have already been published in our Art Series:
Chagall, Matisse, Picasso, Renoir, Toulouse-Lautrec, van Gogh.
All the volumes run to 96 pages and are fully illustrated in colour.
Format: 230×300 mm, softcover.

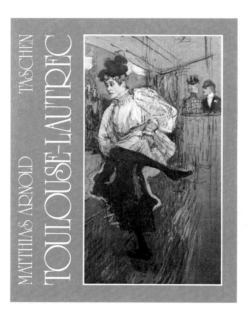

The author and publishers would like to thank the collectors, photographers and archives who have given permission to reproduce the works in this book. For illustrative material we are indebted to: André Held, Ecublens. Archiv Alexander Koch, Munich. Gruppo Editoriale Fabbri, Milan. Piper Verlag, Munich. Matthias Buck, Munich. Ingo F. Walther, Alling. Walther & Walther, Alling. Quotations from van Gogh have been taken from his letters, most of which were addressed to his brother Theo. Special thanks are due to Rainer Metzger and Charly Prestele of Munich for their editorial assistance.